Lamps and Shades

Lamps and Shades

Beautiful ideas to make and decorate

Juliet Bawden

Photography by Jon Bouchier

NEW HOLLAND

For Ray and Ann –
thank you for all your help
with making this book

First published in 1996 by
New Holland (Publishers) Ltd
London · Cape Town · Sydney · Singapore

24 Nutford Place
London W1H 6DQ
United Kingdom

80 McKenzie Street
Cape Town 8001
South Africa

14 Aquatic Drive
Frenchs Forest, NSW 2086
Australia

10 9 8 7 6 5 4

ISBN 1 85368 733 2 (HB)
ISBN 1 85368 761 8 (PB)

Art director: Peter Crump
Photographer: Jon Bouchier
Copy editor: Emma Callery
Stylist: Labeena Ishaque

Editorial direction: Yvonne McFarlane

SPECIAL THANKS

The Publishers and Author would like to say a special thanks to
Fads and Homestyle. BHS for being so generous with their products
and to Mazda for providing technical backup and products.

Reproduction by CMYK, Cape Town, South Africa

Printed and bound by Tien Wah Press (Pte) Ltd, Singapore

Contents

Introduction

I have written this book for a variety of reasons. First of all, I love lamps, for light is something to which we are all drawn automatically. Secondly, creating lamps is an exciting as well as a creative pastime, and many designers throughout the world are producing imaginative new designs for lamps using a wide variety of exciting materials.

This book is first and foremost a lamp and shade book - it is not a lighting book. At the time of writing, no other books are available which solely deal with making lampshades and making and decorating lamp bases. It also provides a wealth of inspirational ideas from many of the new designers who are at work today. Using this book you will be encouraged by other people's designs to make your own lampshades or bases, or you may simply choose to decorate or embellish plain, ready-made department store lamps.

Because taste is such an emotive word and preferred ideas for colour, shape and materials vary, even between people living in the same house, I have included many different styles of lamp within this book. There are shades made from traditional materials such as silk and parchment and others made from more unusual ones such as bark, plaster, embedded bandage, resin, old tea bags, and forged metal. As well as being very different in design and materials, they also range in size from about 2 m (5 ft) down to 30 cm (12 in) and cater for both formal and informal settings. What will look good in the kitchen most likely will not be suitable for a bedroom, and, of course, children and teenagers have different ideas again of what they want in their own space.

The projects in the book are all easy to make and have clear step-by-step photographs so that you can follow them. Some of the lamps, such as the mosaic lamp base on pages 86-89 or the child's fabric lamp on pages 82-85, use recycled materials. I have included three paper lampshade projects – one pleated, one pierced and the third made from cut paper. There is one standard lamp project, and the rest are either wall or table lamps, the latter being the most popular kind of lighting.

The book is also jam-packed with ideas for embellishments and once my assistant, Labeena, and I started dreaming them up, it was virtually impossible to stop adding to our lampshades. For those readers to whom craft means sewing, stitching or painting, and for whom electricity is a rather fearsome idea, do not be put off. The creative possibilities are endless, whether you are doing a very easy paint effect such as sponging the base of a lamp or perhaps sticking images on a shade or just making holes around the edge of a shade with a punch and then threading through ribbon. If you like sewing, we have a most flamboyant chiffon lampshade (see pages 90-93) and even a crochet lamp (pages 72-75), as well as some beadwork (pages 64-67), and lamps made from glass (pages 60-63 and 102-105). This book has lots for you to make without being in the least technical. So, have fun and good luck with your lamp making!

Juliet Bawden

Styles of lamps and shades

Historical overview

Centuries ago, the main source of artificial light was always fire and so the focal point of any room was the fireplace. This state of affairs lasted for many centuries. It is hard to imagine now, but until the mid-20th century, more than half the world's population, especially in the country regions, used fire as the principal light source. For the peasant cultures, this meant that their day was governed by the daylight. People living on the land would rise at break of day and go to bed at sunset. In medieval times in the great halls there would be a roaring fire blazing night and day, primarily for the heat. The light created by these flames would be supplemented by blazing torches held aloft or placed on iron spikes and left to burn. The less well off used rush lighting which consisted of strips of rushes dipped into oil and held in position in a simple iron stand. Oil was not universally available and even this proved too much of a luxury for some households; for them mutton fat was the only alternative.

The predecessors of the candelabrum and the chandelier date from medieval times with floor-standing metal candelabra on whose many arms were spikes onto which candles were placed. Candle-beams, similar to chandeliers, were also common at that time. Suspended from the ceiling, these could hold many candles on wooden arms radiating from a central bar.

Candle power

For centuries, candles were the principal source of light (and, of course, candles are still favoured today, though usually only as a supplement or to produce mood lighting). Soft wax or tallow candles were impaled on spikes for placing on tables while larger versions, created to stand up to a height of 1.5 m (5 ft), contained several candles on one stand. It is recorded that 25,000 candles would be burned in the course of one evening at the 17th-century court of French king Louis XIV at Versailles. It is hard to imagine now, but the level of lighting would have been extremely low, even in those houses where lots of candles were affordable, for it takes 120 of them to produce what would be today the equivalent output to a single, 100-watt electric light bulb.

From the middle ages right up until the 19th century, however, for the ordinary working family candles were a luxury and,

Chandeliers, whether lit or not, were once an important decorative feature in interior design, and much emphasis was paid to their embellishment. The introduction in the mid-17th century of rock crystal, which was beaded and threaded onto wire armatures or linked together into chains to form chandeliers, drew attention to their intricate, reflective structures.

left: Close-up of a Georgian chandelier in the Octagon Room at Bath Assembly Rooms. *(NT Photolibrary/Andreas von Einsiedel)*

above: The magnificent drawing room at Felbrigg Hall, Norfolk, with its fine chandelier and Rococo candlebranches. *(NT Photolibrary/Nadia MacKenzie)*

were smoky, dripped wax, blackened ceilings and walls, were a real threat to safety — and they smelled unpleasant.

Slowly, candelabra became more elaborate in their design and began to be produced in iron and in carved and gilded wood with up to 12 branches. After 1750, wealthier owners of Georgian homes installed candelabra using reflective materials to maximize the illumination produced by candles. It was at this time, too, that raising and lowering of these central lights was introduced and became widely used.

Lanterns were developed during the 18th century and these were either portable or fixed, used both indoors and on carriages by coachmen. Large, oil-burning lanterns using seven or eight candles framed with brass or iron were to be found in great halls and in stairwells while elaborate sconces holding several candles were now being placed on walls. By the end of the 18th century, chandeliers had become huge and very ornate apparently consisting of showers of cut glass which sparkled in the grand Georgian dining rooms.

in addition to fires, their major source of light was rush lighting. It was not until the 16th century that the socket candlestick we know today emerged and this would usually have been made of brass. During the 17th century, there were several types of candle holder: the candlestick, which could be placed on a flat surface; sconces, to be hung from the walls; and chandeliers, suspended from the ceiling. Some of them were so lovely to look at that they evolved into objects of display. But candles had many drawbacks, especially those made from rendered down animal fat known as tallow candles. They

Lighting in America

The term 'colonial' best describes the style of furniture and architecture being produced in North America from the 1650s to 1700. There were, of course, strong regional differences in design, reflecting the different countries of origin and backgrounds of the pioneer settlers. Candleholder designs of the time included stands with small circular tops and tripod bases. There were also iron sconces and plain wrought-iron, Dutch-style chandeliers with wooden centres. From the late 18th to the early 19th centuries, the

Federal style flourished in America, during which period candlelight remained the usual form of lighting. But in keeping with the more formal style of Federal decoration, lighting became more sophisticated in design and, as a result, both candelabra and chandeliers were increasingly decorated with rock crystal drops.

Most American chandeliers were made of polished brass, wrought-iron, or punched tin; early versions held candles, while later examples burned oil. Many kinds of lighting devices were invented and improved in the USA during the 19th century. The increased availability of candles and thin sheets of tin led to thousands of chandeliers being made and used in nearly every American home.

19th-century developments

In Europe, oil lamps became more commonly used during the 18th and 19th centuries when there was a real period of innovation in lighting. Light produced from oil lamps was much more intense than that achieved from candlelight and it was at this time that flues, reservoirs and reflectors were introduced which made oil lamps much more convenient to use. Nevertheless, candlelight was still the most popular system of lighting, especially when a method of hardening wax was discovered at the beginning of the 19th century which meant that there was now far less mess. Scope for designers was greatly enlarged now that illumination became more dependable and cleaner with table lamps, wall brackets and hanging devices developing from the ornate Georgian age to an elaborate fussiness in the early part of Queen Victoria's reign. The use of heavy drapes at this time acknowledged that natural light was less important and put more focus on light gained from the oil burner. Gas lighting did not develop in Europe until the 18th century, despite the fact that the ancient Egyptians, Chinese and Persians had all used this source to provide lighting.

The advent of electrical lighting

With a supply of coal gas piped to wall-mounted gas mantles, it became possible to install fixtures in all rooms in the house, providing a flexibility of supply hitherto unknown. But gas was wasteful and dirty and it could be unreliable, causing furnishings and belongings to be ruined. Yet the advantages far outweighed those produced by candle or oil light and the illumination it provided was up to ten times greater.

The possibility of using electricity as a source of light had been known since Humphrey Davy, an English chemist, first generated electric light in 1809. His invention was inappropriate for domestic purposes because it required a low-voltage supply, so it was initially used only for street lighting, and also for lighthouses from the 1850s. The other requirement was for a better filament to be used in lamps which would last for longer than a two-minute period. It was not until 1878, when Joseph Swan made a carbon filament which meant that the lamp did not catch fire and a year later when Thomas Edison (working independently in America), invented the forerunner to the light bulb used today, that the widespread use of electricity became a real possibility. Both Edison and Swan were marketing their lamps in Britain by 1880 and they decided to form the Edison and Swan United Lamp Company which later became Ediswan. The two inventors

above: An original oil-burning lamp (c. 1880). The base is made from brass and it is fitted with an etched shade and a chimney. Modern equivalents use paraffin as a fuel or they are often converted to electricity.

(Loaned by Mr and Mrs Fare)

had used different methods to connect the bulb to the supply circuit and they remain as standard fittings today — the brass screw-in cap invented by Edison and the bayonet fitting introduced by Swan.

In 1880, the armaments millionaire Lord Armstrong was the first Briton to install electric lighting using the filament bulb in his house, Cragside, in Northumbria, which required its own electricity generators. In New York, Edison patented the first electricity supply network to households in 1882. The popularization of an electricity supply to all households in Britain was eagerly awaited, but before 1900, progress was slow because of the cost of installation, yet with the increase in the number of consumers, this slowly dropped until by 1913 most medium to large houses had electricity. Even so, this still represented only two per cent of the population. It must be remembered that gas supplies were not common either, so at the start of World War I, oil lamps were still the most used form of lighting in Britain.

Lighting had become an issue of class. Those that could afford artificial lighting had it installed and it thereby became a status symbol and very fashionable.

The gas industry, still only in its relative prime, fought back against these new innovations. Welsbach's burner was one of the main weapons used in this fight during the 1890s along with the inverted gas mantle, which produced a shadow-free light. A gas switch was also introduced to rival that used for turning the electric light on and off. Builders were canvassed and offered premiums by both gas and electricity companies to include fittings for piping in supplies to new housing — electric light had now become a major selling point.

New colour schemes

The increased use of electric lighting now led to a change in the way in which houses could be decorated. Paler colour schemes were introduced — these would have been prohibitively expensive to renew on a regular basis up to this point because of the dirt created by the previous methods of illumination — candles and oil and gas lamps.

Lighter colours also helped save on the cost of providing additional light. For example, it required 87 candles to light a room panelled with dark woodwork and painted in dark colours as opposed to the 33 candles which were required to provide equivalent light in the same room whose walls and ceiling were painted white. Even so, lighting levels were still very low in those days, with early electric lamps producing only the equivalent of a modern 25-watt bulb.

In this period when gas and electricity were vying for supremacy, there was obviously great scope for innovative design. The ceiling pendant, introduced for use with candles, was still commonly used either singly or with a crossbar for two gas burners. Adjustable pendants, often placed above the dining table, were used so that light could be directed. It was usual to see wall brackets at right angles to the wall, on either side of the fireplace. These were often hinged so that they could swivel to extend into the room.

Lamp and shade design

The need to increase the general lighting level while also diffusing and softening it led to a change in lampshade design. During the 1870s and 1880s, this consisted of a large glass globe with an open top. But shapes now altered to include rectangular shades which were thought to diffuse light more effectively than a globe, and holophane (prism) shades.

Some designers stuck rigidly to traditional shapes, placing light bulbs on candlesticks for both individual lights and chandeliers. Small shades were now sometimes placed over the bulbs, which had not been possible before. The light bulb was so new that it was often left exposed or incorporated into the design as the stamen of a flower, but this was soon found to create too much of a glare. Fittings began to be adapted to take both gas and electricity supplies; this was advantageous to designers such as William Arthur Smith Benson who worked comfortably with both old and new technologies. Benson eventually took over the crafts-based furnishing company of William Morris in 1896 and developed simple Arts and Crafts-inspired designs using brass or copper with glass for wall lights. His influence was great both at home and abroad, and he recognized the need to create general lighting as well as softer, more diffused effects; in France, Emile Galle was working along the same lines.

During the first decades of this century, numerous styles of lamps could be found illustrated in catalogues of the day. Fittings ranged from classical revival styles and those designs from those of the Arts and Crafts movement to Art Nouveau. In America, Tiffany lamps, made by hand using iridescent Favrile glass, became extremely popular. Louis Comfort Tiffany, whose firm of interior decorators was the most famous in New York, had travelled in Europe, met leading figures from the Arts and Crafts movement and admired their philosophies. Knowledge gained during his travels influenced his

designs and as an innovator of Art Nouveau, led to his success. The Tiffany Studios produced an enormous range of household goods, the most famous of which were the lamps. Tiffany's patented coloured glass techniques and his knowledge of the effects of light led to the design of lampshades featuring naturalistic patterns including peacock feathers or lily pads, for which he is still rightly remembered.

The Edwardian age also had numerous styles of lamps and fittings ranging from wonderful frilly confections for softening the harsh effect of the light bulb to the simplified designs of the Arts and Crafts movement. The curves and subtle colours of Art Nouveau were followed by the more angular Art Deco style with its duller yet bolder colours in the glass shades.

left: Dragonfly lamp made from coloured glass, with coloured glass nuggets embedded between the dragonfly wings; a replica of a Tiffany lamp. In complete contrast to the shade, the base is a heavy bronzed metal twisted into an organic shape. *(Christopher Wray)*

below: A typical example of Art Nouveau, with a semi-clad woman forming the lamp stand, is finished with antique silver lustre. These figurative lamps are given names such as melody, nymph and ecstasy. The shade is in the form of a flower, usually a tulip, lily or bluebell. *(Christopher Wray)*

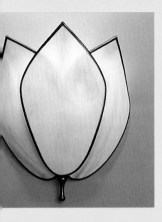

above: A glass up-lighter wall bracket made from opalescent glass. Three overlapping petals create a soft glow and diffuse light across the ceiling. *(Christopher Wray)*

New designs and materials

The years between World War I and World War II produced the most radical innovations in many areas of design and it was at this time that there was, at last, universal domestic electric lighting. This coincided with the rise of Modernism, when new designs, inspired by industrial methods and materials, became functional and less decorative. Bakelite, Formica, chrome and steel were now all used for electric fittings. Track lighting first made its appearance during the Twenties and Thirties and the anglepoise lamp was designed in 1932 by George Carwardine. Six years later, the fluorescent tube first appeared in America and by about 1942, they were beginning to be used in the home. Experiments to extend the life of a light bulb began right from the time they were introduced by Swan and Edison.

After 1907, most bulbs used a tungsten filament, but greatly improved luminosity was achieved when, in 1910, William Coolidge found that he could produce drawn tungsten. It was around this time, too, that the discovery was made about how to vary the mixtures of nitrogen and argon, the gases in light bulbs and bulbs in a variety of wattages began to be manufactured. Yet, it was not until 1964, when tungsten-halogen lamps were introduced, that there were any further technical advances to the quality of lighting.

In 1972, two lamps came onto the market which have become classics and make use of the new 12-volt halogen lamps. These were the Papillon uplighter, which is really a standard lamp that throws light up towards the ceiling, and the Tizio desk lamp, designed by Richard Sapper. The light created from a tungsten filament is a warm, yellow colour and is most often used with hanging fixtures and table lamps. Halogen bulbs provide a white light which is clearer, and built-in reflectors can mean that the light is more controllable and focused.

During the early 1980s, most western economies were buoyant. With populations already interested in household and furniture design, there was a growth of high-profile interior decorators — people such as Ralph Lauren, Osborne and Little, Tricia Guild — who designed lifestyles for the masses, including papers, paints, linens and, of course, lights. At the same time, there was a boom in consumer magazines which promoted new designs and designers. You could at last choose the style that you aspired to, and, what is more, you could live in it.

High style at affordable prices

As with the fashion industry, these designs led to changes in the high streets so that innovative companies such as BHS in Britain launched new ranges of lighting which echoed those of the top designers, but at an affordable price for everyone. In the 1990s, boom turned to slump, house prices fell, unemployment rose, and people could not afford to move home so often.

Despite, or perhaps because of, this there has been a burgeoning of talented designer/makers who are creating interesting accessories for houses, including lights and shades. Many of the designs reflect the softer, more natural, look using home-spun linen, calico and other natural fabrics for shades and soft wood for bases. Other designers go for the brash, brightly coloured, synthetic look of much of the fashion around at the moment. We are lucky to live in a time of such choice.

Gallery

The lamps in this section of the book have been chosen for many different reasons, but most of all, to inspire, to give you ideas and to help you when choosing lamps for your own home. Most of them are table lamps as they are the most popular, but we also show a selection of floor and wall lamps in many different settings. They do not just have to be indoors, but can create a wonderful ambience in a garden room or conservatory, or outside in the garden. It is important that the proportions of a lamp and shade look good together. If you own a few lamps, try swapping around the shades and bases — you might be pleasantly surprised with the results.

Living rooms
classic lamps and shades

With most of us living in smaller houses, flats and apartments these days, rooms often have a duel purpose. Whereas in the past there might have been a sitting room or parlour, and a separate dining room, often a dwelling nowadays will only have a kitchen and living room. This one room may be used for many different kinds of activities from dining to sitting watching television or as the place where homework or hobbies such as sewing might be carried out. The computer, stereo system and television may all be in this room, too. To reflect the number of activities that take place in today's living rooms, this is the largest group of lamps in the Gallery, beginning with some beautifully classic lamps and shades.

above: A coolie shade decorated with a combination of decoupage and ripped papers, gold leaf and bleach. It is set off by a brass candlestick base. *(Shade by Andrea Maflin, base by Fads)*

left: Here is a large ceramic, cream coloured lamp base which would look good in a fireplace or even on the floor. The shade is a pretty embossed paisley pattern. *(Loaned by Ann Scampton and Ray Moxley)*

opposite: The design on this sunflower shade has been painted with gold gutta percha and then decorated with silk paints applied using a brush. The sunflower pattern on the ceramic base is made from a glaze applied before the final firing. *(Shade by Trisha Kerr Cross, Papier Marché, base by Dartington Pottery)*

below: This lamp base is in the style of a classical urn with verdigris winged handles. The shade is made from giselle silk. *(Christopher Wray)*

above: Traditionally hand-made and painted in China these lamp bases are beautiful and depict traditional Chinese images. The shade is Empire shaped. *(Christopher Wray)*

above: The base of this very beautiful lamp is made from green marble and the shade is from paper that has been marbled using oil paints on water.
(Loaned by Ann Scampton and Ray Moxley)

right: An unusual and stylish Danish lamp. The base is made from a dark heavy metal in complete contrast to the white parchment Empire shade.
(Gore Booker)

Living rooms
retro lamps and shades

The past has always provided inspiration for all artists and designers, and lighting is no exception. For the lamps here, you don't need a retro decor to offset the simplicity and kitsch of the designs.

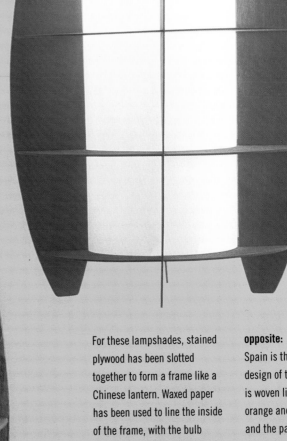

For these lampshades, stained plywood has been slotted together to form a frame like a Chinese lantern. Waxed paper has been used to line the inside of the frame, with the bulb giving a soft yellow-white glow. They can be hung as a pendants or stood as table lamps.
(Furniture Union)

opposite: A holiday to sunny Spain is the inspiration for the design of this lamp. The base is woven like a basket from orange and blue dyed wicker and the parchment shade has been screen-printed with holiday images.
(Robert Wyatt)

above: Standing on very thin, tripod-like legs these shades are extremely simple and pure in their construction. They are made from thick cartridge paper which has been screen-printed with watery stripes in summer fruit colours. *(Fiona McKeith)*

This wrapped red silk shade is shaped like a fez. The stand is made from a thin metal tube which rests on the floor on a flat disc. *(Mr Light)*

below: Kitsch images of bananas and sweets are printed on these utilitarian shades to give them a quirky lift. The shades are made from cartridge paper and the legs are thin bent metal tripods. *(Fiona McKeith)*

above: The lamp on the left is made from four pieces of suede which have been cross-stitched together. The centre lamp was created in the same manner, but is conical and the parchment lamp on the right has a cowboy image screen-printed on the shade. They are all quite typical of 1950s' style. *(Robert Wyatt)*

Living rooms
geometric lamps and shades

The lamps and shades in this section are formed into weird and wonderful, yet very definite shapes. They would all look good in any light, bright interior.

above: On the left, white muslin has been wrapped around a frame and sprayed to stiffen it and to retard fire. On the right, green cotton lycra has been stretched over a wire frame in the same way. *(Furniture Union)*

right: These pendant lights have been made from swimsuit lycra stretched over metal frames. The base of each light has a cast resin point which glows when the lamp is lit. *(Michael Hartley)*

right: A 1.5 m (5 ft)-tall lamp called S-bend. The wire frame is wrapped in raw, slub silk with diamond-shaped decorations. *(Philippa M Rampling)*

far right: Laughing Lucifer, a 76 cm (2½ ft)-high wire-framed lamp wrapped with raw silk, specially imported from India. *(Philippa M Rampling)*

below: Moscow pendant lamps made by wrapping silk around a frame and then spraying with fire retardant. One lamp is finished with a wire spiral, the other with a tassel. *(Mr Light)*

Living rooms
resin lamps and shades

Resin cast lamps give off a beautiful ambient glow when lit. As resin can be cast into virtually any required shape, it is a very versatile material and one which is very fashionable at the present time.

right: The bases on these lamps are made of moulded, highly reflective blue resin. The shades are rough plastic sheeting that has been slotted onto yellow perspex supports. When the lamps are lit, the yellow supports are reflected upon the resin bases.
(Ben Comley)

left: These yellow, conical lamps have the bulb placed in the centre of them so that the whole cone glows when switched on. One of the lamps is set on three little orange cast legs and the other has a resin flower suspended above the lamp on a wire arc.
(Trait d'Union)

above: This mushroom-like lamp is supported on a wiggly metal stand. The shade is cast white resin, giving an even and quite bright light. The green resin starfish along the lower edge are optional - they can be unscrewed and removed.
(Trait d'Union)

opposite: This lamp is very classical in style, yet contemporary in its construction. As well as there being a bulb underneath the shade, there is also one set inside the base.
(Trait d'Union)

above: The bulb for this lamp is placed inside the base so that most of the light given off comes from the base rather than the shade. *(Trait d'Union)*

Living rooms
folded and twisted lamps and shades

Twisted and folded lamps are made by using malleable materials which can be formed when heated and then shaped and joined by riveting. The lamp and base is often made as one element. They can be made from a number of different materials including plastics (which can be moulded), or ply-wood, first used in the early 1950s for making chairs.

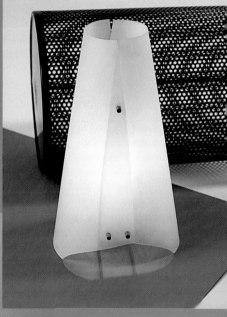

above: This lamp is made by heating and forming a frosted perspex sheet which is then held together with hand-turned brass rivets.
(Caroline Bromilow)

opposite inset: Recycling objects to create a lamp is creatively challenging as well as environmentally sound. The results can be amazing, easily fitting into your living room.
(Junior Phipps)

left: Bent plywood was the new material in the early 1950s and it is having a revival in the 1990s, as this lamp shows. Note how the perforations create pin pricks of light.
(Caroline Bromilow)

right: These wonderfully eccentric lamps are made from various twigs, pods and soft woods, which have been sculpted into curly shapes. The shades, created from barks and dried vegetable skins, are lit with tiny bulbs.
(Karen McBain)

Hallways

The lighting by the front door and the hallway in a house is important for several very functional reasons. If your entrance is well lit, you are less likely to trip up or be attacked, and you will be able to see to find your keys. Good lighting in a hall will also create an instantly welcoming impression as part of an arrangement alongside, say, fresh flowers and a mirror, or the lamp may be stunning enough to make a statement all of its own.

above: This lamp is Oriental in design and is set off beautifully by its silk pleated shade and the Chinese bowls and plates. *(Base loaned by Ann Scampton and Ray Moxley, shade by Christopher Wray)*

right: This globe base made from tulip wood has been decorated using distressed gold leaf on a base of red oxide primer. The shade is a combination of decorated and torn papers and decoupage. *(Base by Lilli Curtiss, shade by Andrea Maflin)*

right: This is a very modern looking lamp and shade. Both were purchased from a department store and then customized to fit in a modern hallway. The base is painted with acrylic paints, the shade with fabric colours. *(Juliet Bawden)*

above: This elegant, pleated silk shade stands on a plaster column base that has been decorated with leaves and then gilded. *(Christopher Wray)*

Studies

A study is usually a place for contemplation and work of a more studious nature, so while any table lamps chosen for these rooms do not have to be serious, it is probably better that they are not too distracting. It is important that good task lighting also is provided to prevent eye strain. Halogen bulbs provide the nearest illumination to natural daylight.

above: This black lacquer-like candlestick base is decorated with an heraldic symbol. The shade is made from a highly reflective vinyl material. *(Loaned by Ann Scampton and Ray Moxley)*

left: Cayenne pepper in colour, this study is warm and womb-like. The table lamp reflects this mood in both the shade and base. The shade is made of pleated silk, the base is a twisted carved candlestick decorated in a pretty floral design. *(Christopher Wray)*

left: The parchment-coloured walls of this study act as a foil to the richness of the artifacts within it: a lacquer chest with a gilded decoration and a lamp made from a tea caddie in black with gold and a shade to match. *(Loaned by Ann Scampton and Ray Moxley)*

above: This swan-like, long-necked lamp is made from corrugated paper which has been treated with fire retardant. This lamp is, in fact, made by a hat designer who has created hats using the same technique. *(Claudette Chapeau)*

Bedrooms

Lampshades play a key role in decorating schemes, especially in a bedroom, where you want to be comfortable with the light. The size and shape of the lamp and shade are important design decisions, and will have to be taken into consideration along with the size of the room and the proportions of the other furnishings. The colour and texture of the material chosen to make the shade will directly affect its appearance and the quality of the light given out. Translucent and lightweight fabrics give off a warm glow, whereas heavy fabrics in strong, dark colours tend to throw the light directly above and below the lampshade.

above: This squat lamp base has an indigo design, with the colour of the line encircling the top of the base reflected in the wrapped and twisted shade. Different thicknesses in the wrapping produce an interesting diffusion of light. *(Base loaned by Ann Scampton and Ray Moxley, shade by Charlotte Smith)*

left: A pair of pretty lamp bases made from glazed ceramic and decorated with a Chinese blossom design. The pleated shades produce a warm glow suitable for a bedroom. *(Loaned by Ann Scampton and Ray Moxley)*

This large china base with flattened concave sides has a large coolie shade giving an elegant finish. This lamp throws out a deep pool of light when switched on. *(Loaned by Ann Scampton and Ray Moxley)*

Children's rooms

As long as all safety precautions are taken (see page 122), choosing lamps for children's rooms is a great opportunity for having fun. Lamps can be shaped like animals or carry a theme such as a nursery rhyme. As a word of caution, only buy children's lamps from a reputable company, as many cheap imports do not live up to required safety standards.

below: "The cow jumped over the moon". Here is a sweet lamp depicting the nursery rhyme Hey diddle diddle. A resist gutta outline is painted on the shade and then filled in using fabric paints. The base is a block of wood which has had a central core drilled into it to carry the flex. *(Trisha Kerr Cross, Papier Marché)*

above: This soft wood snail lamp is very simple in construction with two circles making up the shell shape. The light fitting is simply screwed onto the back of the snail image. *(Shui Kay Kan)*

right: This paper lamp has been decorated with three-dimensional wire figures, some of which are attached to the paper and others embedded into it. The orange paper exudes an orange glow when lit. *(Shui Kay Kan)*

Inside/outside

Lamps can play a significant role in inside/outside living. Conservatories are becoming more and more popular and are often added as an afterthought to a house. Entertaining may take place here and this is a fine opportunity for some unusual lighting.

left: Two floral floor lamps made from patinated metal. The bases are stem-like with leaves attached. The lamp on the left is in a flower pot filled with pebbles sunk into concrete. *(Eryka Isaak)*

above: These lamps are made from oxidized beaten copper and mounted on a base of slate or embedded in concrete. The lights are cones of frosted glass and the shapes are all organic in origin. *(Eryka Isaak)*

left: Pig light sculpture. This is a variation on the theme of the ubiquitous Chinese lantern, except this time instead of a globe the paper is formed into the shape of a pig. The artist who created this lamp also makes dogs and other animals. *(David Page)*

right: These standard lamps are made from bamboo canes embedded in a plaster base. The shades are made from waxed paper and a hole punch used to make holes along the edge of the shades to join together the elements with twine. Pieces of twig bamboo are laid horizontally across the shade for decoration. *(Yuko Suzuki)*

Creating lamps and shades

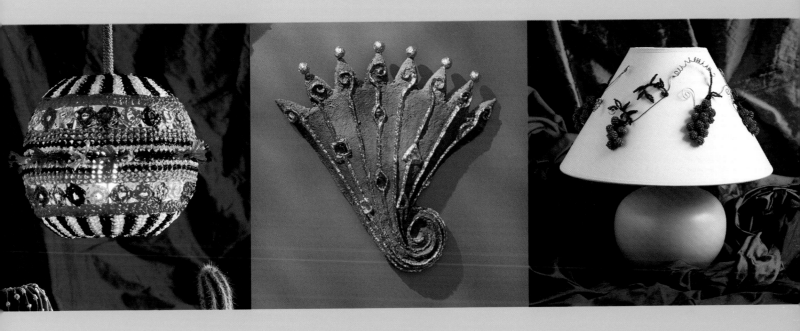

Pleated lampshade

There is such a huge selection of gift wrapping papers around that the basic idea of this shade can be adapted to fit in with absolutely any surroundings, from a child's wrapping paper to the most sophisticated gold tissue paper. The only thing to be aware of is that the tissue paper should be quite thin and light enough to allow the light and the images on the wrapping paper to show through. Because the tissue paper is actually laid over the wrapping paper, the image may become slightly obscured. But as soon as the lamp is turned on, the image on the pleated shade is revealed. So, with just a sheet of wrapping paper, some tissue paper, glue and deft handy work, you too can make these striking pleated lampshades. Use a ribbon of a contrasting or matching colour to give that tied-up and finished touch. *(Designer: Karen Triffitt)*

MATERIALS & EQUIPMENT

four 50 x 70 cm (20 x 27 in) sheets
tissue paper

wallpaper paste · paintbrush

50 x 70 cm (20 x 27 in) sheet
wrapping paper

cloth · scissors · pencil

ruler · clear adhesive

paper clips · hole punch

darning needle

1 m (1 yd) of 6-18 mm (¼-¾ in)-wide
ribbon

lamp base and stand

opposite: A pretty collection of pleated lampshades made from layers of paper. When the light is on, the images on the decorated paper are diffused through the plain paper on top. *(Karen Triffitt)*

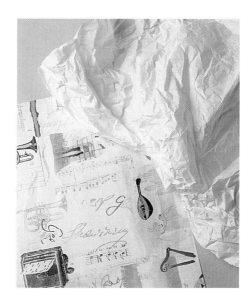

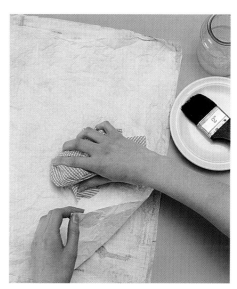

1 Scrunch up sheets of tissue paper very well to create creases in them, then unfold and, using the wallpaper paste, stick two layers of tissue paper onto the right side of the wrapping paper.

2 Flatten the layers together with the cloth, to prevent tearing. Set aside and leave to dry for about an hour.

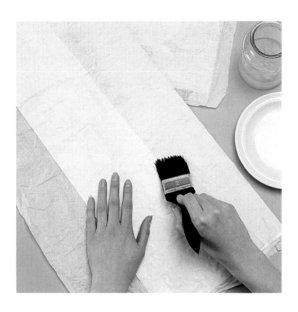

3 Cut the paper, in half lengthways. Then stick a sheet of the remaining tissue paper onto each half. Stick them on top of the previous tissue layers, leaving an overlap along each long side. Stick the overlaps onto the wrong side of the wrapping paper and leave to dry. This gives a neat, strong edge.

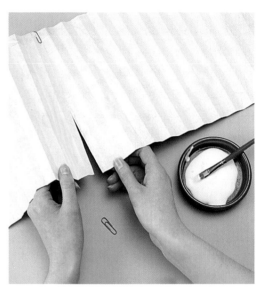

4 Trim off any excess tissue with the scissors. Turn to the wrong side and on each piece of paper mark pencil dots at 12 mm (½ in) intervals along both the top and bottom edges. Join the dots using the ruler and pencil to make the parallel lines that will act as a guide for pleating both sheets of the paper.

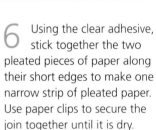

6 Using the clear adhesive, stick together the two pleated pieces of paper along their short edges to make one narrow strip of pleated paper. Use paper clips to secure the join together until it is dry.

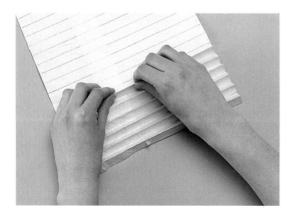

5 Pleat one sheet of the paper, folding it neatly along the pencil lines and keeping the folds evenly spaced. Fold the second sheet in the same way.

7 Using the pencil, mark where to punch the holes by making
dots 12 mm (½ in) in from the top edge in the centre of each
pleat. Then mark another row a further 2 cm (¾ in) below that but
this time through the fold of each backward facing pleat. Using the
hole punch, punch all the holes around the lampshade.

8 Stick together the remaining two narrow
sides to form a tube. Then use the darning
needle to thread the ribbon through the top row
of holes. Pull the pleats together.

9 Place the lampshade on the frame and adjust
the ribbon until the pleats fit the top edge of
the frame, and the lower set of holes grips the top
wire support. Finish the shade by tying the ribbon
into a pretty bow.

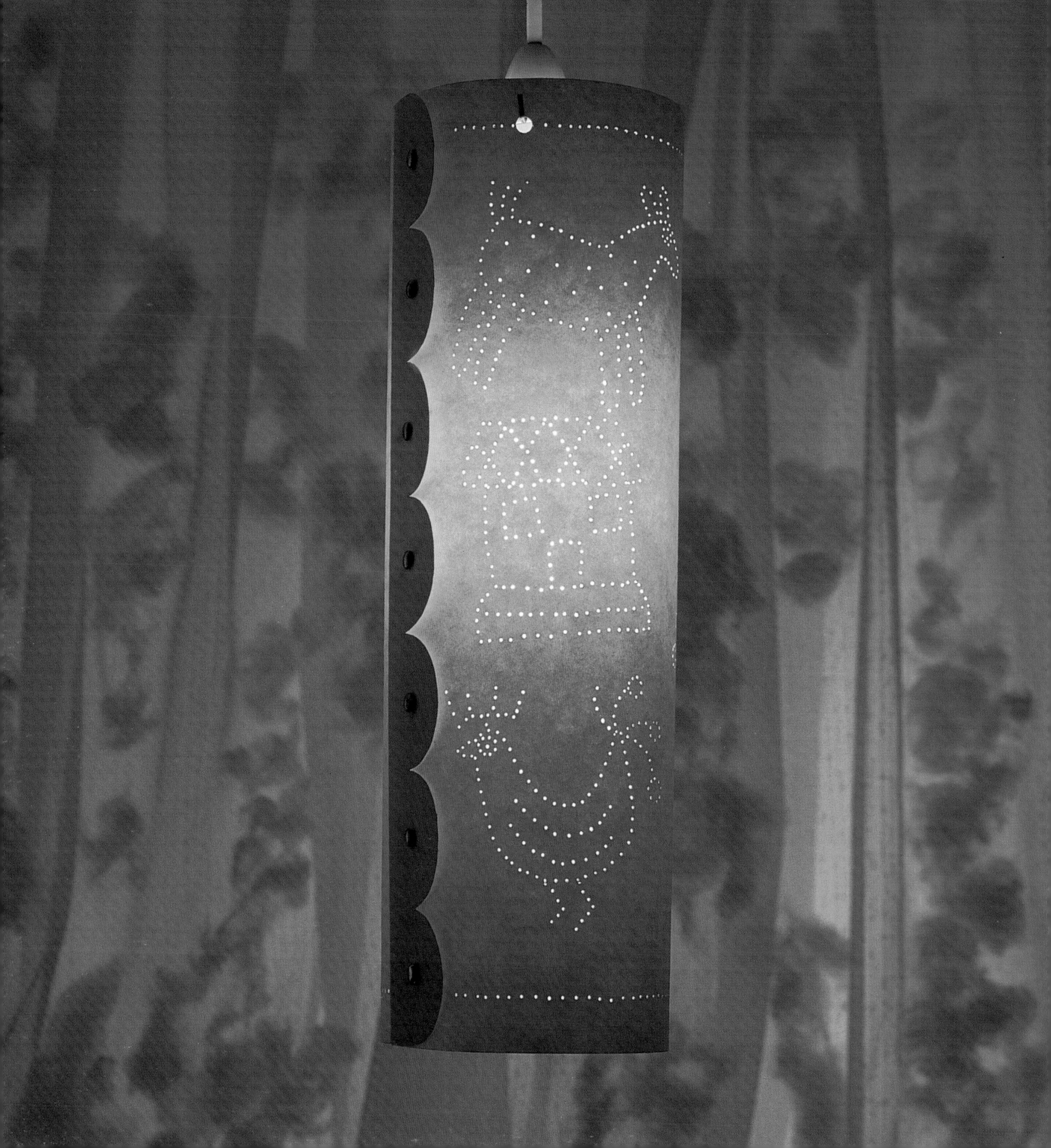

Pin-pricked suspended paper lampshade

The light that emits from this lampshade largely depends upon the type of paper you choose to make it with. Light will travel through translucent, natural coloured parchment paper giving a soft glow. Here, the parchment has been pin-pricked with simple patterns to create subtle differences where the light shines through the paper and through the holes.

Simple figurative images have been chosen that are very child-like and naive in design. More complicated images will not have the immediate effect that these naive figures have. Ensure that the pin pricks are close enough together so that the designs can be clearly seen but that they are separated sufficiently so that they don't look messy. Use the pattern given here or vary the image at will to suit your decor.

(Designer: Deborah Schneebeli-Morrell)

MATERIALS & EQUIPMENT

sharp pencil

30 x 34 cm (12 x 13 in) sheet thin white paper

plastic pot lid or similar circular object

37 x 42 cm (14½ x 16½ in) parchment paper

small pointed scissors

cutting mat · bradawl · metal ruler

paper clips · hole punch

7 brass paper fasteners

brass spider fitting

bulb holder · electrical flex

20 watt energy-saving light bulb

opposite: A simple device for creating star-like patterns in a shade is to pierce it with a pin. This simple naive design is made by drawing animals onto paper and then transferring their outlines by making holes in parchment paper beneath. *(Deborah Schneebeli-Morrel)*

1 Draw your pin prick designs onto the thin white paper. Make them as simplistic as possible so that they will clearly show up on the finished lampshade. The motifs used on this lampshade are given overleaf so if you wish to use them, trace the outlines onto the thin white paper.

2 Using the small plastic lid as a template, draw semi-circles with the sharp pencil along one of the shorter edges of the parchment paper. Using the sharp scissors, cut along the pencilled semi-circles making a scalloped edge.

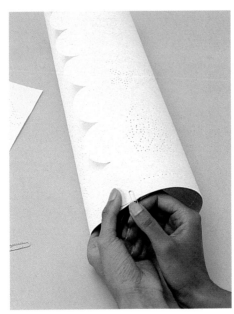

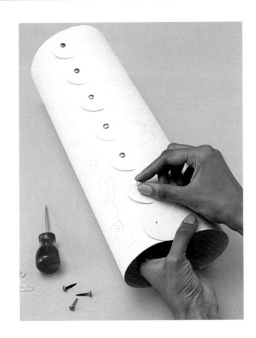

3 Lay the parchment on a cutting mat or a thick magazine and then place the sheet of pin-prick designs centrally over the parchment. Begin to punch through the lines with the bradawl, approximately four holes to 12 mm (½ in). Also pin-prick a border line 2 cm (¾ in) in from the top and bottom long edges.

4 When you have completed pricking out the design, remove the design paper. Then mark off the centre of each scallop with the pencil and roll the parchment around onto itself so that the scalloped edge overlaps the straight edge. Secure the parchment temporarily at both ends with a couple of paper clips.

5 With the bradawl, make a hole through the middle of each scallop on the pencil mark and through the paper behind the scallop. Push paper fasteners through the holes and open out inside the shade.

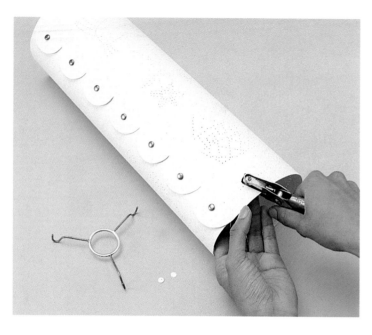

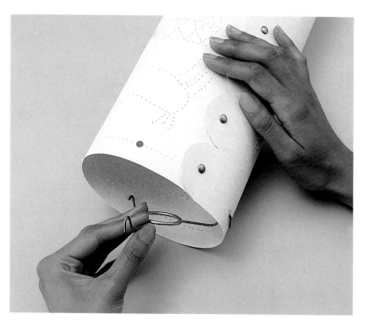

6 With the hole punch, make three evenly-spaced holes 2 cm (¾ in) from the top of the shade along the line of pin pricks.

7 Insert the brass spider fitting through the holes made in step 6. Then position the bulb holder and flex, suspend the light and insert the low-energy bulb.

Standard lamp and shade

An old standard lamp has been transformed by the addition of a new shade and some emulsion paints mixed in bright colours. The colours used here aren't regular colours that are available from shops, but you can have colours mixed to your specification at a DIY store. On the lampshade, use acrylic paints as they flow very easily on parchment.

For design inspiration, look at things around you, especially items with surface pattern, such as wallpapers, tiles and curtains. For this project, an old papier mâché urn was used to give ideas for the pattern that was eventually painted onto the base and shade. The stars intertwined with ropes have been used as they are flexible to paint; as the pattern is not symmetrical, mistakes can be easily rectified. If you first paint the base with white emulsion it will give a clear background to start work on. *(Designer: Juliet Bawden)*

....
MATERIALS & EQUIPMENT
....

standard wooden lamp base

sandpaper (fine grade)

emulsion paints (white, various bright colours)

paintbrushes (medium, fine)

pencil (soft)

acrylic paints (various colours)

large parchment shade

opposite: An unusual and modern looking lamp and shade were created by sanding off any varnish, painting a base coat in white emulsion and then decorating in brightly coloured patterns. *(Juliet Bawden)*

1 Sand the wooden lamp base thoroughly with the fine grade sandpaper, to prepare it for the primer.

2 Prime the base with white emulsion paint. For a smooth and even finish, use two to three coats allowing each to dry before painting on the next one.

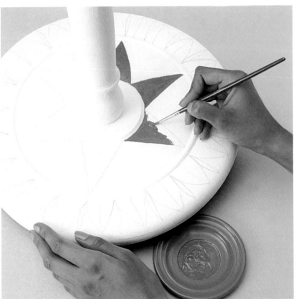

3 Draw your design onto the base with the pencil. Here I first drew on the star and then added further details like the rope and feathers using a vase as the inspiration for my design.

4 First paint the larger areas of the design in your chosen emulsion colours. Wash your paintbrush thoroughly between colours to keep your design crisp and clear.

5 Then paint the smaller details, using the fine paintbrush and contrasting colours.

6 To decorate the parchment shade, first draw your design lightly onto the shade, again with the soft pencil.

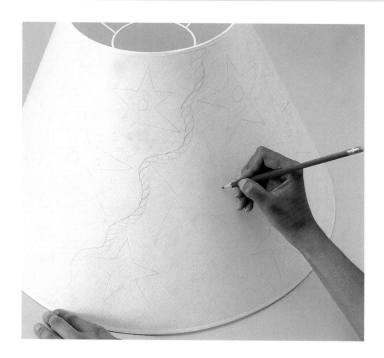

7 As with the lamp base, fill in the design using the acrylic paints and fine paintbrush.

Cutwork lampshade

Paper must be one of the most versatile materials for lampshade making, as well as one of the most inexpensive, ranging as it does from hand-rolled Japanese cartridge paper to Egyptian style papyrus paper, textured and stringy tissue paper to velvety embossed paper.

The concept for the detailing on this shade is similar to that of an advent calendar in that the orange paper, which is used for the main body of the lamp, is scored with a number of systematically placed crosses. These are then opened out to create little square windows, revealing light through them, like uncurtained house windows. The cut shade project shown here has the added interest of being lined in a contrast coloured and textured handmade paper, so that the light seen through the windows has a soft and dappled glow. *(Designer: Cheryl Owen)*

MATERIALS & EQUIPMENT

drum lampshade frame
rough paper · masking tape
pencil · ruler
fine handmade paper (yellow)
scissors · all-purpose adhesive
medium-weight paper (orange)
cutting mat
large paper clips
dressmaker's pins
craft knife

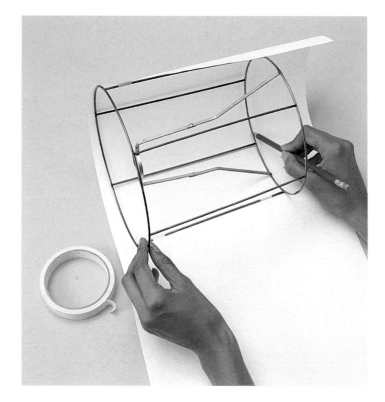

opposite: These shades are simple and inexpensive to make, yet look so sophisticated. The orange card with the yellow tissue paper revealed through the cut-out windows gives a warm and welcoming glow from a crisp outline. *(Cheryl Owen)*

1 To make a template for the lampshade, start close to a vertical strut and wrap a sheet of rough paper around the frame joining together sheets of paper with masking tape if necessary. Hold the paper smoothly in place on the frame with pieces of masking tape. Overlap the paper where it meets. Then draw around the frame above the top of the rim and below the lower rim. Mark the position of the struts and overlapped edges.

2 Carefully remove the template and lay it out flat on your worksurface. Add 1.5 cm (⅝ in) to one overlapped end and add 1 cm (⅜ in) to the top and lower edges. Then cut out the template. Draw four 3 cm (1¼ in)-wide bands that are evenly spaced across the template and centred to the depth. Draw a 3 cm (1¼ in) square within each band between the struts, alternating the position of the squares.

4 Again using the template, cut the lampshade from the medium-weight paper and lay the it on the cutting mat or a thick magazine. To indicate the position of the squares, hold the template firmly on the back of the paper using the paper clips and pierce each corner with a pin.

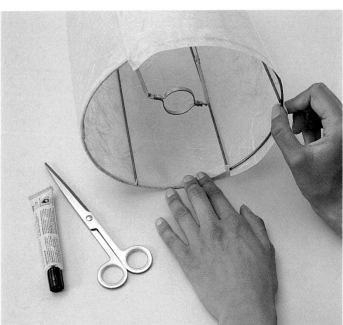

3 Use the template to cut the lampshade from the handmade paper. Wrap the paper centrally around the frame, overlap the ends and stick together. Fold the top and lower edges over the rims, snipping the paper occasionally so it lies smoothly, and stick in place.

5 Using the craft knife, carefully score the paper between the pin pricks, marking out each square. Then cut diagonally between the corners, making a cross. Gently depress the square to poke the cross outwards.

6 Wrap the paper smoothly around the handmade paper, overlapping the ends. Stick the overlapped ends together and hold in place with the large paper clips until the adhesive has dried. Dab a little adhesive along the top of the frame's rim to secure the shade in position.

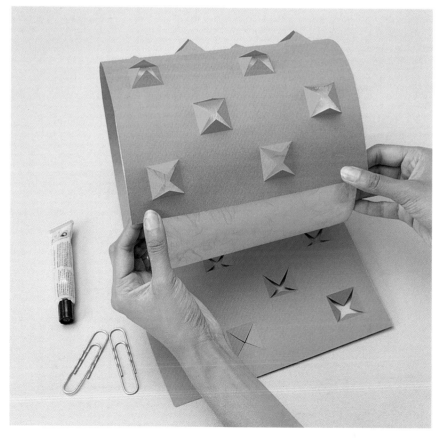

Riverside painted glass lampshade

This clever lampshade uses a combination of soldered and painted glass panels interspersed with sections of a pleated lampshade to make a very pretty bedtime lamp. Plain sheets of glass are outlined with a fake lead effect paste and then filled in with translucent glass paints to produce a stained-glass effect. The glass panels have then been slotted into position around the top and bottom support rings of the lamp-shade frame. Michael Ball has used a selection of blues and pinks to create a relaxing, riverside ambience and when the light shines through them it has a soft, watery-like glow. The contrast of the glow of light through the glass panels and the quite sharp light through the pleated sections is stunningly effective. *(Designer: Michael Ball)*

MATERIALS & EQUIPMENT

pleated lampshade supported on a frame with vertical bars

tape measure

scrap paper · pencil · ruler

3 mm (⅛ in) float glass

5 m (5 yd) of 6 mm (¼ in)-wide copper foil

scissors · wire

round nosed pliers

1 small bottle flux · paintbrush

1.5 mm (¹⁄₁₆ in) diameter brass or copper wire

soldering iron (75 watts or more)

1 stick 50:50 tin:lead solder

contour paste

glass paints (blue, pink, white)

artist's paintbrush

roller blind fray check (optional)

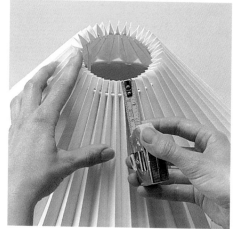

1 Measure the width of three pleats around the top edge of your lampshade. Repeat with the bottom edge of the lampshade and note down the measurements on a piece of paper.

2 Then measure from the top to the bottom of the shade and use these measurements to draw a template on a piece of paper which you will use to make the glass panels. Draw a line from top to bottom on the template in the centre and also mark the position of the wires that run around the lampshade near the top and bottom. These will ultimately act as a guide for positioning the hanging hooks. Next, using the paper template, ask a glazier to cut five pieces of the 3 mm (⅛ in) float glass to this size.

opposite: A lovely lampshade incorporating paper pleats and painted glass panels, in a variety of soft blues. This and the chiffon-wrapped shade (see pages 90-3) are probably the two most feminine lampshades in the project section of the book, and they have both been designed by men. *(Michael Ball)*

3 Then add the copper foil. This is sticky on one side and comes on a paper backing. Remove part of the paper backing and position one edge of a piece of prepared glass in the centre of the foil. Work your way around the glass, covering all the edges with foil in the same way, making sure that the overlap is always even. When you get to where you started from, cut the foil so that there is a 6 mm (¼ in) overlap. Very carefully push down the sides and rub them with a piece of wood or a pencil to make sure the foil is smooth and well stuck. Make neat corners by folding in the foil at the edges.

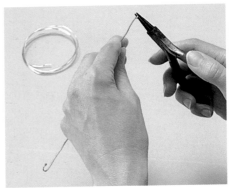

4 Cut ten 15 cm (6 in) lengths of the wire and bend a small hook at each end of each piece.

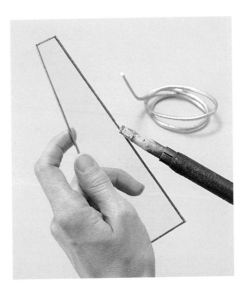

5 So that the solder will stick to the foil and run smoothly, paint on a coat of flux to the copper foiled edges. Plug in the soldering iron about 5 minutes before you need it and then melt a bead of solder onto the soldering iron and run it along the fluxed foiled edges until they are covered in a thin layer of solder. Also coat the wire hooks with clear solder.

6 Apply flux to the wires and tinned copper foil edges and, using the template as a guide, solder each hook so that they are positioned by the top and bottom lampshade ring lines. Hold the other end of the wire with the pliers as you solder it in place — about 2.5 cm (1 in) of soldering will be sufficient — and then cut the wire just below the point where it is joined onto the foiled edge.

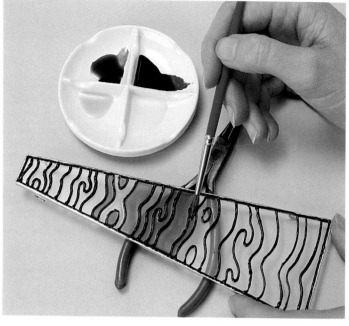

7 Ensure that each panel is well supported and apply contour paste across the glass in wavy lines, as in the photograph above. To make it easier to apply regularly, draw the design on paper first and trace over it onto the glass. Leave the paste to dry before painting (about 10 minutes).

8 Paint the glass using glass paints. Use as many or as few colours as you like. Here, Michael Ball has used a limited number but he has mixed in white in various quantities to give a wider range of shades. Allow 24 hours for the paint to dry.

9 Remove the shade from the frame and fix the completed glass panels onto the lampshade frame using the hooks to hang them in place. Then cut the shade into sections that are wide enough to fit between the five, evenly spaced, glass panels. If the shade begins to fray when cutting it, spray it with the fray check.

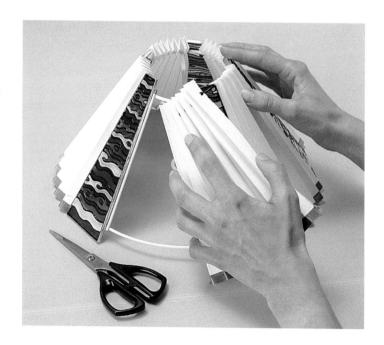

Grapevine lampshade

A bedside lamp is made over, ambrosia style, into lighting fit for a Greek God with bunches of luscious grapes scattered over its surface. Wooden beads are covered with tiny purple rocaille beads using a needle and thread which are then gathered into bunches of grapes. The foliage is similarly created by threading green rocaille beads into strings and tying them to look like vine leaves. Finally, bent gold-plated wire tendrils and the leaves and grapes are sewn onto the shade.

Adapt this idea to create bunches of cherries, raspberries and straw-berries, depending on your taste in fruits. Or make many different coloured balls, attach them to copper wire and sew onto the shade in an abstract design. *(Designer: Debbie Siniska)*

MATERIALS & EQUIPMENT

60 pea-sized wooden beads

nylon monofilament thread

100g (4 oz) size 10/11 purple glass rocaille beads

100g (4 oz) size 10/11 green glass rocaille beads

beading needle

1 sheet A2 cartridge paper · pencil

4 m (4 yd) 1 mm (1/24 in)-diameter gold-plated wire

round-nosed pliers

lampshade and base

scissors · sticky tape

1 The wooden beads are covered with the small rocaille beads. To do this, take 1 m (1 yd) of the nylon thread and tie a knot around the first purple glass rocaille bead, leaving a tail of 30-38 cm (12-15 in). Using the beading needle, thread a further 5 glass beads onto the nylon; then take the needle around and up through the centre of the wooden bead, so that the glass beads lie around the curved surface of the wooden bead. Repeat in the same way until rows of rocaille beads cover the surface of the wooden bead. As you work around the bead, you will need to reduce the number of beads that you thread on. Cover enough wooden beads to make four bunches of grapes.

2 To form the main stem, thread up one of the covered beads' tails and pick up about 7.5 cm (3 in) of green rocaille beads. Then form a leaf on the end by picking up another ten beads (in the same colour) and pass your needle back down the ninth bead to form the leaf tip. Then pick up eight (in the same colour) to complete the leaf shape and pass your needle down the whole stem, at the point of the first of the ten you picked up for the leaf. With your working thread, make a knot here and there onto the stem thread.

opposite: An extremely simple bedside lamp, available from any department store, has been given a new lease of life with rocaille beads forming bunches of grapes to hang on the shade. *(Debbie Siniska)*

3 To form the second stem (this time with no leaf), thread up the tail of one of the covered beads and pick up five green rocaille beads. Take the thread through one of the rocaille of the main stem (at approximately eight beads up from the main stem covered bead), and back through the five rocailles of the second stem; passing the needle on through the centre of the covered bead. Knot off and take the thread back into the beadwork. Repeat this process, working up the main stem. For the last three beads, take the thread into the main stem bringing the thread out just below the leaf, and form three more leaves, in the same way as you made the first one.

4 Draw a lampshade template on the cartridge paper to fit your lampshade (see page 123). Then use the design outline given opposite — or design your own — to draw your vine design on the paper marking the positions of the bunches of grapes and spiral tendrils. Next, using the round-nosed pliers, bend the gold-plated wire to match the design.

5 Place the template over the shade and using double lengths of the nylon monofilament thread (knot at one end), start to sew on the wire stitching using stab stitch through both the cartridge paper and the shade.

6 Sew on the grapes in exactly
the same way, bunching them
up as you work. Once the stitching
is complete, very carefully cut away
the paper to reveal the original
lampshade beneath.

Papier mâché wall light

Pulped papier mâché is extremely versatile and can be moulded into almost any shape. Here, Ann Frith has made large shell-like wall shades by moulding the papier mâché over clay and tin foil. Once the main body of the shade has been made, the piping details are added. Only when the shade has dried completely is it painted, and then the decorative touches added – gold leaf on the piping and precious gems to add to the sparkle.

When making the mould for the shade, remember to ensure that it stands far enough away from the wall so that the bulb fitting can fit inside and there is also sufficient room between the shade and the bulb.

(Designer: Ann Frith)

....

MATERIALS & EQUIPMENT

....

clay · board on which to work

kitchen foil · paper

PVA adhesive

sponge · sharp knife

sandpaper (fine grade)

emulsion paint (white)

acrylic pigment (light blue)

paintbrush · Dutch gold leaf

acrylic varnish

glass blobs · epoxy resin

small wall bracket

light fixing

low-energy bulb

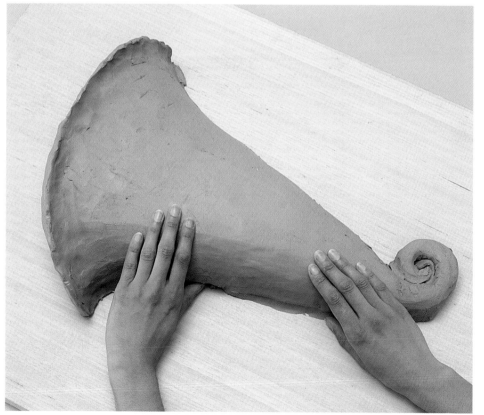

1 Using the photograph opposite as a guide, form a shell-like shape from clay on a flat worksurface or board. This will be used as a mould for the papier mâché shell.

opposite: Inspired by the designer's love of sea life, these sumptuous shell wall shades reflect the colours of the sea off-set by jewel gems and gold leaf piping. The method used for making these shades can be put to good use to make matching accessories like boxes, paper weights and ornaments. *(Ann Frith)*

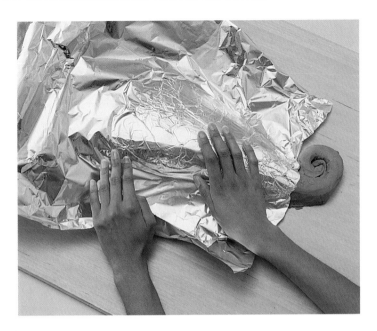

2 Cover the main body of the clay shape in a large piece of kitchen foil and the curly end piece in another piece of foil. Press them firmly onto the clay so that any decorative detail shows through. Then make the papier mâché pulp. Soak strips of paper in water overnight. Then boil the paper strips in water for 20 minutes and liquidize the pulp, adding more water so that the blades of the blender will turn easily. Squeeze out excess water and mix the paper pulp with PVA adhesive until smooth. (Mix a 1 litre [2 pt] bowl of pulp with 175 ml [6 fl oz] of PVA adhesive.)

3 Cover the silver foil shape, with the clay still beneath, in papier mâché, smoothing it on with your hands so that the pulp is even all over. To add the decoration, squeeze the pulp into shapes and press onto the lamp base. The PVA in the pulp will adhere the decoration to the base. Leave the lampshade to dry which will take up to five days depending on how warm the environment is. To speed things up, put the shade in a warm airing cupboard.

4 Carefully remove the clay shape but leave the foil in place behind the paper mâché lampshade (it will protect the paper and stop the lamp overheating). Clean the foil with a sponge and water. Trim and sand the edges of the lamp.

5 Mix the white emulsion paint with some of the coloured acrylic pigment and paint the lamp all over.

6 Cut the Dutch gold leaf into 1.5 cm (⅝ in)-wide strips. Then cover the part you want gilded with PVA and press the Dutch gold transfer paper onto the adhesive. Paint the gold leaf with clear acrylic varnish to seal. Finally, stick on the glass blobs using epoxy resin.

Note: When fixing this light to the wall make sure the bracket holds the light away from the shade. Also, use a low-energy bulb which will not overheat.

Crochet raffia pendant lampshade

This lamp uses an old-fashioned material, raffia, and an old-fashioned technique, yet produces quite an esoteric and modern result. The colours used are vivid and very South American in theme; bright pinks, purples, yellows and oranges. When you buy raffia in such colours it tends to have a really glossy sheen, giving an even more unusual effect. Rachel Howard Marshall crochets in a very contemporary manner and produces an exciting pendant shade.

The shade should be crocheted to the exact measurements given here, so it will stretch over the pendant shade frame otherwise it will hang too loose or become mis-shaped. Because the crocheting has a very loose weave it is recommended that you use a low-wattage bulb, otherwise the bulb light will tend to glare through the holes.

(Designer: Rachel Howard Marshall)

MATERIALS & EQUIPMENT

2 skeins (44 m [48 yd]) artificial raffia in white, black and red

1 skein (22 m [24 yd]) artificial raffia in light green, orange, bright pink, pale pink, bright yellow, pale yellow, purple, lilac, dark blue, light blue, bright green and dark green

crochet hook (size 3.5 mm)

large eyed needle · scissors

round pendant lampshade frame with 12 struts (diameter: 20 cm [8 in], height: 18 cm [7 in])

Abbreviations

beg	beginning
ch	chain
dc	double crochet (single crochet)
htr	half treble (half double crochet)
rep	repeat
sl st	slip stitch
sts	stitches
tr	treble (double crochet)

1 This lampshade is crocheted in several parts: top and bottom (two separate pieces, each alike), rings of decorative circles (two separate rings, each alike), and a central strip.

To make the top:
Using white raffia and the crochet hook:
10 ch, 1 dc in 2nd ch from hook, 1 dc in each of remaining 8 chs, 1 ch, turn.
1 sl st in each of first 3 sts, 1 dc in each of next 3 sts, 1 htr in each of last 3 sts.
Change to black raffia.
* 1 ch, turn, 1 dc in each st (9 dcs in total).
1 ch, turn, 1 sl st in each of first 3 sts, 1 dc in each of next 3 sts.
1 htr in each of last 3 sts.
Change to white raffia and repeat from *.

Continue to repeat from * alternating black and white raffia until you have a total of 36 stripes (18 black and 18 white). This should be long enough to fit tightly around the top part of the lampshade frame. Overstitch the first white stripe to the last black stripe to form a ring and sew in all ends. With red raffia, crochet a row of sl sts around the lower (wider) edge of the black

and white crocheted ring (approximately 72 stitches).
Sl st in first st at beg of round.
* 1 ch, 1 dc in each st.
Sl st in first dc at beg of round.
Rep from * 1 more time.
Cast off and sew in ends.
Repeat all of step 1 for the bottom piece.

opposite: A round crochet raffia pendant shade reminiscent of Mexico in its bright and hot colours, and bold patterns. It has been created by crocheting the shade in sections and then sewing them together. For added effect, wind a gold cord around the wire. *(Rachel Howard Marshall)*

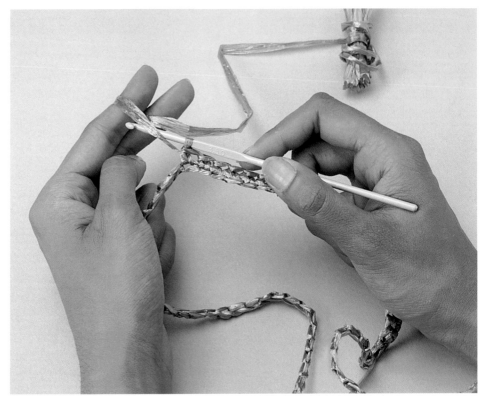

2 For each ring of decorative circles, make 24 circles, each alike. To do this, select 12 colours of raffia and make two circles in each colour, as follows:

4 ch, sl st in first ch to form the circle.

To close the circle: 1 ch, 8 dc into ring, sl st in first dc.

Cast off, leaving a 30 cm (12 in) end of raffia. Overstitch each circle together to make a large ring of circles. Do not cut the ends of raffia yet.

Repeat to make a second ring of circles. Then attach each ring of circles to the last row of red crochet on the shade. Overstitch using raffia ends which are still attached to each circle. Do not cut the ends of raffia yet.

3 To make the central band: Using light green raffia work as follows:

To form a ring: 84 ch, join with a sl st at beg of ch.

Row 1 1 ch, 1 dc in each st, sl st in first dc at beg of round.

Row 2 Work as for row 1.

Row 3 Change to black raffia, work as for row 1.

Row 4 Change to yellow raffia, work as for row 1.

Row 5 Change to black raffia, work as for row 1.

Row 6 Work as for row 5.

Row 7 Work as for row 4.

Row 8 Work as for row 3.

Row 9 Change to orange raffia and work as for row 1.

Row 10 Work as for row 9, cast off and sew in all ends.

For the tufts on the centre band cut 22-26 lengths of various coloured raffias, each measuring approximately 40 cm (16 in).

For each tuft, take a length of raffia, fold it in half and then in half again.

Insert the crochet hook in the centre band, between rows 5 and 6, bring end of hook out again 1 st away from where it was inserted.

Hook the centre point of the folded raffia and pull through to form a four stranded loop.

Hook and pull the ends of the raffia through the loop.

Pull them tightly upwards to form a tuft and trim to 1.5-2 cm (⅝-¾ in).

Repeat all the way around the centre band, inserting each tuft about 2 cm (¾ in) apart.

4 To finish, stretch the centre band over the lampshade frame to cover the middle section.

Place the top shade on the upper half of the frame, using the ends of raffia that are still attached to keep it in place. Overstitch each circle from the top shade to the green crochet on the centre band. Cast off and sew in all ends. Place the bottom shade on the lower half of the frame and attach as for the top shade. Overstitch each circle from the lower shade to the orange crochet on the centre band. Cast off and trim all ends.

Using the white raffia, overstitch the top and lower edges of the crochet shade to the top and lower edges of the lampshade frame.

These two raffia lampshades have been made in a much more straightforward way by wrapping a single colour of raffia around tall frames. *(Skylon)*

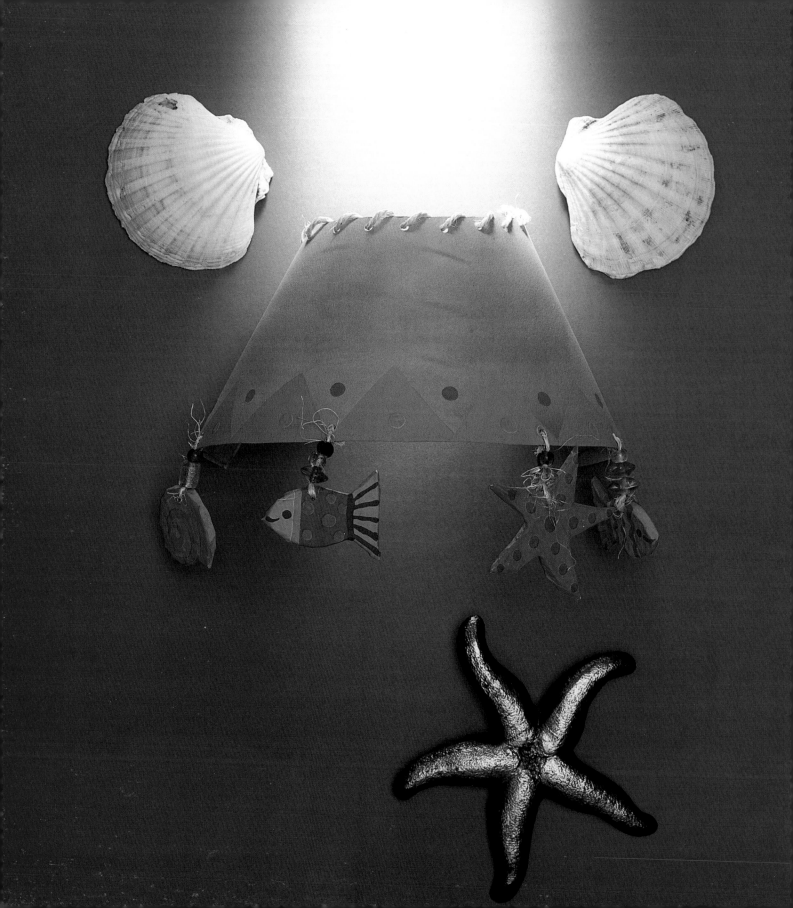

Sealife wall shade

This paper wall shade is a celebration of sealife. The soft blues and greens, the fish and the fisherman's string are all influenced by the designer's love of the sea. This is an inexpensive, very original wall light made from paper, cardboard and decorated with beads. The fish attachments are cut from corrugated cardboard covered in newspaper and then painted in pretty colours. They are tied onto the shade body with a hairy string. The materials used in this project can be found around the house and are very safe, so making it an easy shade for adults to make with their children. This is an attractive shade for children as it has a cartoon-like quality about it. *(Designer: Helen Musselwhite)*

MATERIALS & EQUIPMENT

1 sheet heavyweight watercolour paper
pencil · scissors
8 mm (⅓ in)-thick battening wood
drill · drill bit · metal ruler · hole punch
water-based paints (various colours)
paintbrushes · craft knife
heavy duty stapler · 1 ball 2-ply string
strong adhesive · corrugated cardboard
newspaper · wallpaper paste · bradawl
selection glass beads
2 screws and rawl plugs

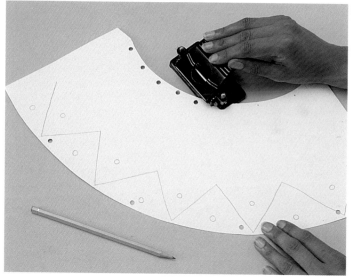

1 Decide upon the size that you would like your lampshade to be and then using a photocopier enlarge the template given on page 79 as required. Position the photocopy of the template onto the watercolour paper, draw around it and carefully cut out. Cut two wooden battens to the size of the straight edges of the lampshade. Drill and counter-size a hole a quarter of the way down each batten (these will ultimately be used to fix the lampshade to the wall).

2 Draw the design onto the shade lightly, with the pencil. Then punch holes along the top and bottom edges for the string and fish decorations. The holes on the upper edge should be closer together than those on the lower edge.

opposite: A simple wall shade, where the embellishments make it so different. For the decorative edging, holes have been punched along the top and bottom and string has been wound around the top, and used to attach little papier mâché motifs around the bottom. *(Helen Musselwhite)*

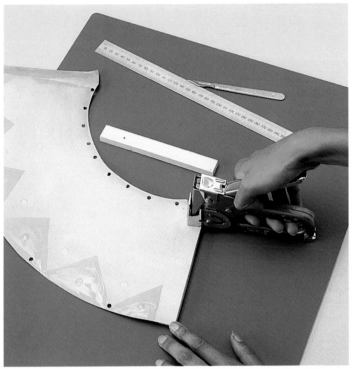

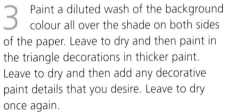

3 Paint a diluted wash of the background colour all over the shade on both sides of the paper. Leave to dry and then paint in the triangle decorations in thicker paint. Leave to dry and then add any decorative paint details that you desire. Leave to dry once again.

4 With the metal ruler and craft knife, score a line 2 cm (¾ in) in from the straight edges of the shade. Fold the paper inwards and securely staple a wooden batten onto it on the wrong side. Repeat with the other edge.

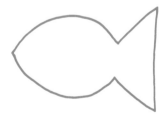

left and right:
Templates for the shell, fish and star fish motifs to hang from the lower edge of the shade. Enlarge the outlines to the size required on a photocopier and transfer onto cardboard.

5 Thread the string around the top edge
of the shade and secure each end with
a dab of strong adhesive.

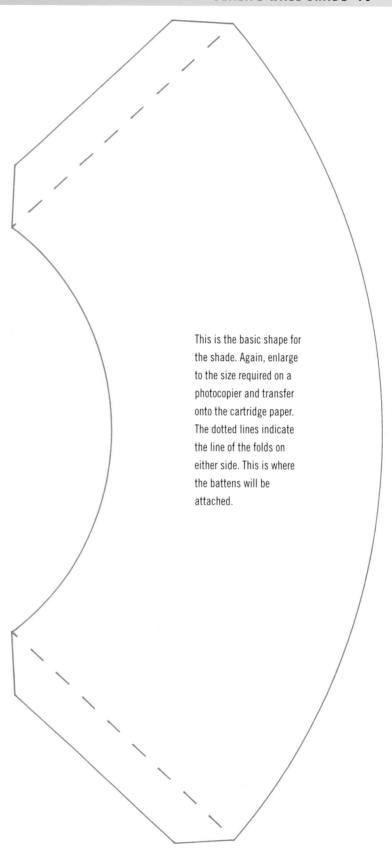

This is the basic shape for
the shade. Again, enlarge
to the size required on a
photocopier and transfer
onto the cartridge paper.
The dotted lines indicate
the line of the folds on
either side. This is where
the battens will be
attached.

6 Cut out fish and other sealife shapes from the cardboard. Cover with torn pieces of newspaper which have been soaked in wallpaper paste. Apply several layers to each shape and leave to dry overnight.

7 Pierce a hole into each piece with a bradawl and paint in your chosen colours. Thread the shapes onto the string and beads.

8 Attach each shape to the bottom edge of the shade (where the holes were pierced in step 2), knot the string and secure at the back with a dab of strong glue. Secure the shade to the wall around a light fitting. To do this, put the rawl plugs into the wall at the appropriate places. Then push the screws through the shade where it is stapled onto the battens and through the previously made holes in the battens and screw into the rawl plugs.

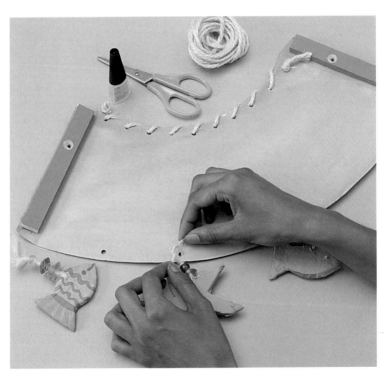

A ceramic uplight wall shade is given an abstract look by painting it in rich blue emulsion and then adding details of squiggles and swirls in brightly coloured acrylics. *(Juliet Bawden)*

A variation on Helen Musselwhite's sealife shade. The same basic shade is used, but it has been covered in large and cheerful gingham daisies that have been glued onto the base. *(Helen Muselwhite)*

Sweet dreams lampshade

This lampshade is made of recycled rags tied to the top and bottom of a wire frame. It costs virtually nothing to make as you will be sure to have rags in your home already. Collect rags in complementary colours so that you can have soft stripes, or tie them onto the frame in strict colour sequences to make striking patterns. If you want to go a step further, you can even weave into the rags once they are tied onto the frame, or thread beads onto the rags. Another variation is to tie wider strips of fabric onto the frame and then stitch them together horizontally using big blanket stitches and bright coloured thread. *(Designer: Debbie Siniska)*

MATERIALS & EQUIPMENT

torn rag strips · scissors

wire frame

crochet hook

4 m (4 yd) 1 mm (¹⁄₂₄ in)-diameter
gold-plated or brass wire

pliers

netting (black)

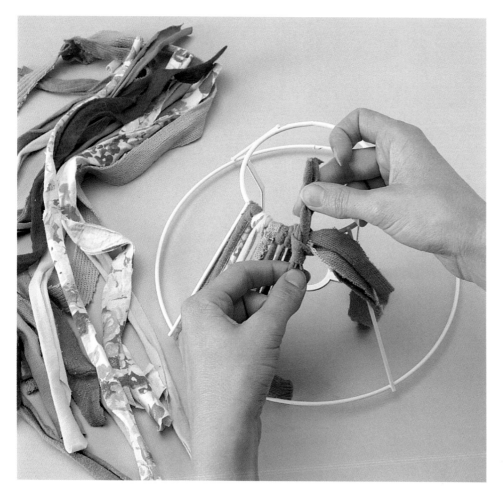

1 Cut or tear a number of 50 cm (20 in)-long and 5 cm (2 in)-wide strips from old items of clothing. Also tear four 70 cm (28 in)-long strips to bind the spirals. Tie one of the 50 cm (20 in) strips around the bottom of the frame and up onto the top ring. Tie the next strip around the loose end of the first strip on the bottom ring and do the same where it joins the top ring. Continue tying the strips in this fashion so that the loose ends are hidden in the knots of each consecutive strip. Use the crochet hook to pull loose ends to the back of the frame. Work your way around a quarter of the lampshade.

opposite: This lampshade is a must for those who cannot throw anything away and are intent on recycling everything and anything. An old lampshade frame is covered in rags and fabric remnants. *(Debbie Siniska)*

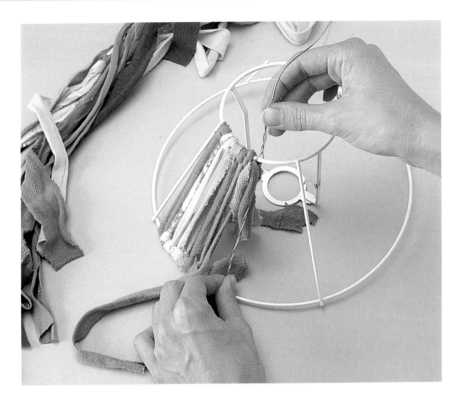

2 Cut a piece of the wire to approximately six times the height of the frame. Bend it in half and place the base of the frame in the bend. Twist the two halves up to the top half of the frame.

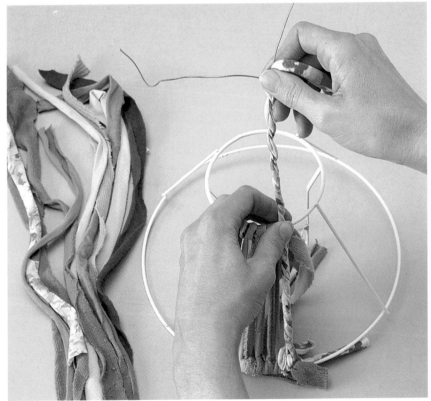

3 Tie one of the 70 cm (28 in)-long strips of fabric to the base of the wire and wrap it around the wire until you reach the top edge.

4 To form a curved spiral at the top, twist the fabric and wire together. When you have done enough to make the spiral, bend the wire and the fabric back down, and continue twisting so that the wire holds the fabric in place. Trim off any excess fabric with the scissors and cut the wire with pliers. Bend the wired fabric into the spiral shape. Repeat steps 1, 2 and 3 until the entire lampshade is covered with strips of fabric and there are four wired spirals evenly spaced around the lampshade.

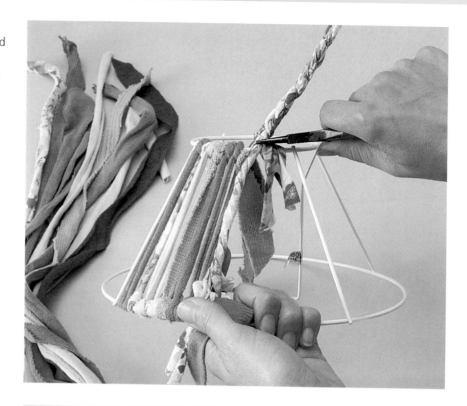

5 Finish by cutting small scraps of black netting and then tying them to the fabric strips to make bow shapes scattered all around the lampshade.

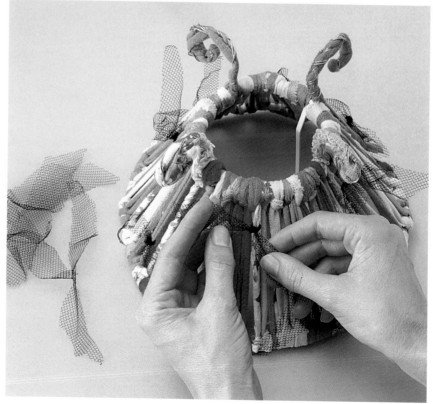

Mosaic and breeze block lamp

This larger-than-life lamp base has a truly Mediterranean feel to it. Helen Baird has been inspired by the works of artists like Gaudi and Gaugin for the exotic sultry figures standing around the base. Mosaic is so very easy to do, and the choice of colours alone can give a strong feeling of place. For example, dark blues and whites look very Roman, and — as used here — turquoise, terracotta and white give a southern European feel.

If you are going to make a large heavy lamp such as this one it must be securely attached to the ground so that it will not topple over. As it can be quite messy to make, you will also need a lot of space, preferably outdoors. You will probably need quite a big room to put it in when you have finished, especially if you are working to this exact size. However, you could make a smaller version if you think it is too big and will overpower your room. *(Designer: Helen Baird)*

....
MATERIALS & EQUIPMENT
....

3 breeze blocks · drill

large masonry bit · cement

4 x 10 cm (4 in)-long metal plates
with drill holes

4 screws · screwdriver · chalk

hammer · tiles · old cloth

tile adhesive

thick gloves (optional)

clean cloth · light fitting · plug

button polish

2 Cement together the three blocks, end to end passing the lamp flex through the central hole just prior to cementing. Then, to ensure that the blocks are well and truly joined together, screw on the metal plates. Screw them on oppsite sides. First you will need to scrape away some of the breeze block so the plates will sink into it and not stand proud.

1 Drill a hole through the centre of each breeze block. This will ultimately hold the lamp flex.

opposite: A mosaic lamp base is created by stacking and cementing together three breeze blocks and adding broken tiles onto its surface. The base is quite tall, measuring 132 cm (52 in) and is perfect for huge rooms and verandas. *(Helen Baird)*

3 Using the chalk, draw the mosaic design onto each side of the blocks. You can at first sketch out your design onto a piece of paper, amending it as necessary until you are satisfied that it looks right.

4 Break up the tiles using the hammer. To ensure that bits don't fly everywhere, wrap up the tiles in an old cloth and bang through that. The more you hammer them, the smaller the pieces become. Working on one part of the block at a time, cover the area with tile adhesive and stick on the broken pieces of tile. Because of the sharp edges it is best to wear thick gloves.

5 When the whole design has been worked, leave it to dry overnight and then wipe more tile adhesive thickly over the surface, filling in between the spaces.

6 Using a clean cloth, rub off the surplus adhesive. Then insert the light fitting into the top of the lamp stand and fit the plug onto the end of the flex. Rub button polish onto the tiles to finish.

right: The mosaic pieces of this wonderfully organic lamp are made from tiny pieces of coloured perspex. They have been stuck onto a moulded fibreglass shell, giving a subtly translucent finish.
(Jane Morrell)

Chiffon wrapped lampshade

This gorgeous lampshade is a wonderfully feminine concoction of gathered chiffon, layered and gathered with a silky lining. It is embellished with rosettes made from left-over chiffon, and velvet ribbon in a complementary colour has been attached along the top and lower edges as the perfect finishing touch. The shape of the frame used here gives this lampshade a particularly stylish feel, but the design works on different shaped frames, too.

The glamour of movie star and Hollywood icon Audrey Hepburn in *Breakfast at Tiffany's* and *My Fair Lady* is evoked in this haute couture look for your living room. It is such an extravagant design it would make a wonderful hat, one that even Givenchy would be proud of.

To estimate the amount of binding tape that is required, measure the length of all the wires, then allow 1½ to 2 times this amount of binding tape. *(Designer: Robert Wyatt)*

MATERIALS & EQUIPMENT

lampshade frame

12 mm (½ in)-wide lampshade binding

50 sq cm (½ sq yd) white lining fabric

tape · dressmaker's pins · pencil

dressmaker's scissors

sewing machine (optional)

needle · threads (white, red)

2 m x 50 cm (2 yd x 20 in) net or chiffon

2.5 m (2½ yd) ribbon or trimming

strong adhesive

tassels (optional)

1 Bind the entire frame — both the top and bottom rings and each of the supporting struts — with the binding tape. Bind the side wires first, leaving one unbound and then bind around the top ring, down the unbound wire and then around the bottom ring. To attach each length of binding, cut off a length of tape 1½ times the length of a strut, turn 2.5 cm (1 in) of tape over the top ring and down the strut. Then wind the binding diagonally over the overlap and down the strut to the bottom. Finish with a knot and trim off excess tape. Repeat for each part of the frame. When binding the top and bottom rings, make a figure of eight with the tape each time you come to a vertical strut.

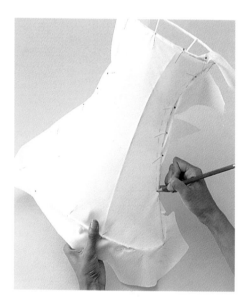

2 To make a pattern for the lining fabric, stretch the white lining fabric over half of the frame and pin in place at regular intervals. Draw a pencil line around the frame on the outside, reducing the size slightly on the vertical edge. Also mark the position of the vertical struts on the fabric.

opposite: These frilly and frothy shades attached to kitsch fifties wicker bases emanate the most wonderful romantic light giving any boudoir a touch of class. *(Robert Wyatt)*

3 Carefully remove the pins and then the fabric from the lamp frame and cut around the pencil line, leaving a 1 cm (⅝ in) seam allowance on the top and bottom edges and at each side seam. Snip the fabric around the curves to allow for a better fit. Cut another piece of lining fabric to match for the other half of the frame, and finally sew the side seams together, right sides facing. Use either the sewing machine or make neat hand-sewn stitches. Trim the seams.

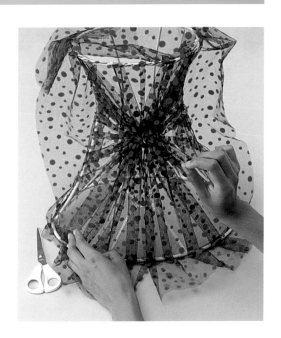

4 Take the netting and run a row of basting stitches along one of the long edges. Make sure the stitches are loose and that one end is firmly knotted in place. Then pull on the other end to gather the netting. Repeat with a second piece.

6 Position the netting around one half of the frame and pin it in place at the top and bottom, rearranging the central gathering if you need to. Overlap the raw edges over the top and bottom edges then hand stitch the fabric all around the edge of the frame. Repeat the process with the second piece of netting on the other half of the frame and trim off any excess netting to neaten.

5 Gather the basted stitches together very tightly to pull the netting into a circle. Fasten off the ends to ensure that the gathering does not come undone. Repeat with the second piece of netting.

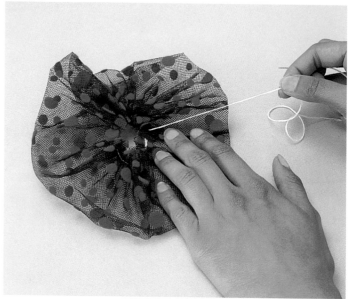

7 Insert the lining into the frame, with the right side of the fabric on the inside. Stretch the lining inside the frame and then hand sew along the top and bottom edges onto the frame. Trim off excess fabric.

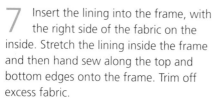

8 Use the excess fabric trimmed in step 6 to make a rosette for the front of the shade. Fold it in half lengthways, baste loosely along the fold, as before, and gather into a rosette, securely tying together the thread ends.

9 Stitch the rosette into the centre of the netting where it is gathered. Then stick on the binding around the edges. For a tidy finish, do the vertical edges first so that the binding on the top and bottom covers the ends. For extra details, sew on tassels in the middle or add an extra layer of chiffon between the lining and the netting in a complementary colour. When the light is switched on, this colour will then shine through the net.

Sheep lampshade

Being Welsh, Melanie William's inspiration for this lamp was the environment of her homeland, of which sheep are an integral part and an animal for which she has a soft spot.

Although this lamp looks difficult to make, it is actually very simple and needs no specialist material to produce. The actual sheep is papier mâché made in the easiest way possible by scrunching up newspaper and taping it into shape and then applying papier mâché over the form. It is then painted and splattered to give an irregular finish to the paint. The sheep figure forms the base for the lamp, and a cardboard tube is used as a lamp stand.

The shade is shop-bought, but has been embellished with small frolicking sheep along the lower rim. Made from furry material, the fabric has been stuck onto the shade with the sheep's heads and limbs painted on in the appropriate place. *(Designer: Melanie Williams)*

MATERIALS & EQUIPMENT

newspaper · masking tape

flour · water · bowl · skewer

paintbrushes (artist's and stiff)

cardboard tube · PVA glue

sandpaper (fine grade)

emulsion paint (white)

acrylic paints
(black or dark brown, cream)

polyurethane varnish (matt or gloss)

fire retardant

lampshade (green)

woolly pile fabric (cream)

scissors · cable · light fitting · plug · bulb

opposite: This innovative lamp base for a shop-bought shade is sweet and quirky, a must for all those sheep fans out there. It is made from papier mâché, so it will be important to spray it with fire retardant before using it.
(Melanie Williams)

1 To form the sheep's body, screw up pieces of newspaper into balls and stick them together with long strips of masking tape. Twist up four newspaper tubes and attach to the main body to represent the legs.

2 Mix up the flour and water to make a thick paste. Tear more pieces of newspaper into narrow short strips and proceed to layer papier mâché onto the sheep's body and legs. You may need to add lumps of paper to help form the animal. Leave the paper to dry between layers. Cover the sheep all over, until it is smooth.

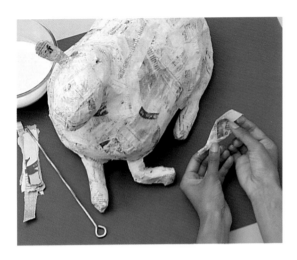

3 To make the ears, take a piece of paper and fold into a sheep ear shape. If you are unsure as to what this looks like, look at a picture of a sheep. Cover with a few strips of papier mâché to neaten. Then make a small hole in each side of the sheep's head using the skewer and insert the ears, neatening with a layer of papier mâché. Leave in a warm place to dry.

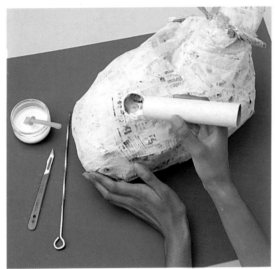

4 To make the hole for the cable to go through the sheep, take the skewer again and bore a hole through the body, making the exit hole towards the back of the sheep to allow the cable to come out. This may take time, but continue to twist the skewer. Once you have made a basic hole, enlarge it using paintbrush handle. Draw around the bottom of the cardboard tube onto the sheep where you have just made the flex hole. Cut out the hole and insert the tube, sticking it in place.

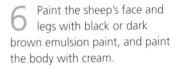

6 Paint the sheep's face and legs with black or dark brown emulsion paint, and paint the body with cream.

5 Smooth down the surface with the fine grade sandpaper. Then prime the model with white emulsion paint and leave to dry once more.

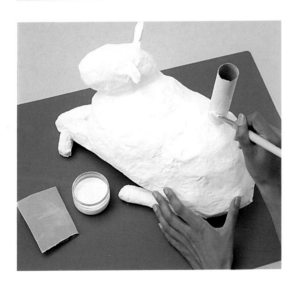

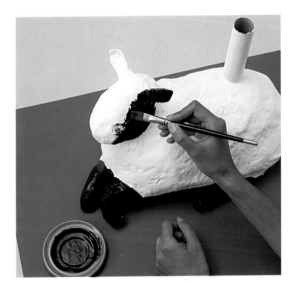

7   To make a more realistic, less sterile sheep, use sandpaper to lightly distress the paint. Also splatter other natural colours onto the body using the stiff paintbrush. Paint on one or two coats of the polyurethane varnish. The number of coats you apply depends on how tough a finish you want to create. Leave the varnish to dry between coats and finally spray with fire retardant.

8   To decorate the lampshade choose a suitable pile fabric from which to make the sheep. Cut out sheep-shaped pieces and stick them around the edge of the shade turning under the edges as you go. Paint each sheep's legs and head.

9   Insert the cable through the hole, attach a plug at one end and a light bulb fitting to the other. Stick the fitting into the top of the hole and finally attach the bulb and shade.

Gold globe lamp

This spherical base is made from turned tulip wood. Dutch metal gold leaf has been glued onto it and then distressed slightly to give an antiqued look. Although this particular base is tulip wood, your choice can be of any kind of wood or any shape, depending on availability and personal preference.

The shade started life as a plain white coolie, which has been transformed into a precious looking object by the same process of applying metallic leaf, though in this instance it is aluminium. Again, it has been rubbed softly to give a textured finish, to complement the base. An unusual and stylish lamp like this is extremely simple to make if you have the correct materials; transform a Cinders of a lamp into a Cinderella, belle of the ball, lamp. *(Designer: Lilli Curtiss)*

....
MATERIALS & EQUIPMENT
....

lamp base

oil-based red oxide primer

paintbrushes (small artist's, large artist's for size, soft for leaf)

3-hour oil size

Dutch metal gold leaf · cotton wool

ormolu cellulose varnish

parchment paper lampshade

PVA adhesive

aluminium metal leaf

clear matt acrylic varnish

1 You can gild onto all sorts of bases as long as they are not porous. If you are gilding onto a porous surface, however, you will need to seal it first. This base is made from turned tulip wood and it has been sealed with a coat of the oil-based red oxide primer. Use a small brush as this means you will get a smoother finish. Leave the red oxide to dry overnight or according to the manufacturer's instructions.

2 Using the large artist's paintbrush, apply a coat of the 3-hour oil size, and leave it to dry. This may take between 2½ and 3 hours, according to the temperature in which you are working. To test if the gild is ready, slide your finger along the surface; if it squeaks it is ready.

opposite: Although the artist who made this lamp had the base specifically made for this purpose, any shop-bought wooden base can be used. The colour of the original lamp does not matter as it will be covered in gold leaf.
(Lilli Curtiss)

3 Pick up a sheet of the Dutch metal gold leaf with either your hands or a paintbrush and place it onto the surface of the base. (Real gold leaf is too fine to pick up with your hands, so if you are using that, you will have to do it with a brush.)

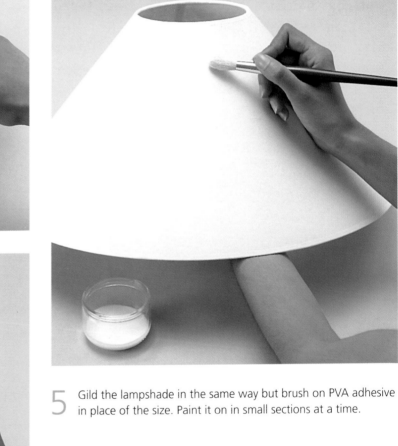

5 Gild the lampshade in the same way but brush on PVA adhesive in place of the size. Paint it on in small sections at a time.

4 Use small balls of cotton wool to rub away any excess leaf and to smooth it onto the lamp. Once the lamp is gilded it has to be sealed or the leaf will oxidize (blacken). To do this, paint on a coat of the ormolu cellulose varnish. Do not use a white spirit varnish as this reacts unfavourably with the oil-size. When the varnish is dry, wire up the base, unless it is already wired.

6 Without leaving the adhesive to dry, press on the aluminium leaf using your hand. Then brush over the leaf with the soft brush to remove sections of the aluminium leaf. Repeat this process until the lampshade is covered.

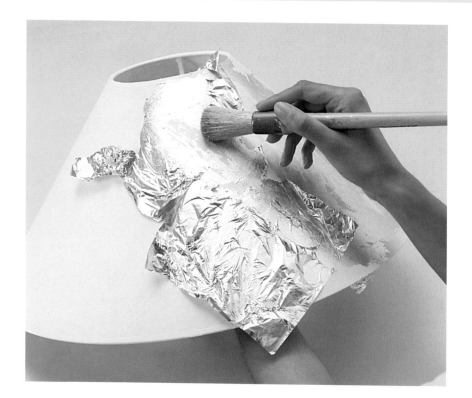

7 To finish, seal with the clear matt acrylic varnish, which will prevent the aluminium leaf from discolouring. The varnish will look cloudy as it is put on but will dry to a clear finish.

Stained glass wall light

This lovely wall lamp was designed in the Art Deco style with a selection of different coloured opalescent glass. Opalescent glass isn't transparent, so when the light is turned on it gives off a soft glow. However, if you prefer a different kind of glass, a wide selection is available from stained glass suppliers (as is solder flux). There are two main kinds of glass: antique and rolled.

Antique glass is mouth blown and comes in many different colours. It is quite expensive and if you haven't worked with glass before it is probably best to work with an inexpensive glass first. New antique glass is similar but because it has been produced by a machine it is cheaper than real antique glass. Rolled glass is also machine manufactured, and there are two types: the opaque opalescent glass as used in this project, and cathedral glass which is transparent and coloured.

This design by Lynette Wrigley is so simple that any of these glasses would be suitable although if you use clear glass the bulb will be clearly visible when the light is switched on. *(Designer: Lynette Wrigley)*

....
MATERIALS & EQUIPMENT
....

opalescent glass (light amber)

semi-opalescent glass
(dark green, streaky amber)

carborundum stone

1 roll of 6 mm (¼ in)-wide copper foil

soldering iron (75 watt minimum)

1 small bottle flux · flux brush

500 g (1 lb) solder

scissors · masking tape

30 cm (12 in) strip tin plate

felt-tipped pen · tin snips

small glass or ceramic dish

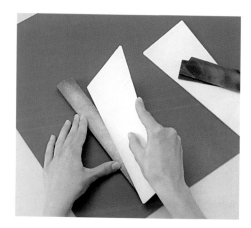

1 Ask your stained glass supplier to cut the glass to the dimensions marked on the template on page 105. Then take the sharp edges off each piece of glass by rubbing each side along the carborundum stone. This gives a key for the foil and removes the sharpness. Wash all the pieces of glass to remove any dust and then dry with a towel.

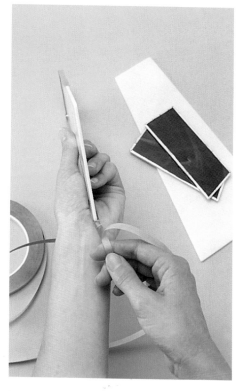

2 Copper foil is sticky on one side and has a paper backing. Remove part of the paper backing and position one edge of a piece of prepared glass in the centre of the foil. Work your way around the glass, covering all the edges with foil in the same way, making sure that the wrap around the edges is always even. When you get to where you started from, cut the foil so that there is a 6 mm (¼ in) overlap. Very carefully press down the sides and rub them with a piece of wood or a pencil to make sure the foil is smooth and well stuck. Make neat corners by folding in the foil at the edges.

opposite: An Art Deco-style lampshade, crafted from glass, suitable for indoor and outdoor use. It has a soft and welcoming glow and would look especially good in an Art Deco entrance hall. *(Lynette Wrigley)*

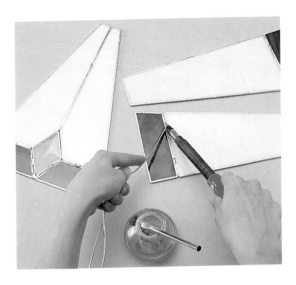

3 Turn on the soldering iron 5 minutes before it is needed making sure it is not touching any surface that it could burn. Assemble the front by applying a blob of flux at intervals along each of the copper foiled seams where the glass joins onto another piece. Tack the joins together with solder over the flux by melting a blob of solder with the iron onto the fluxed joints. Repeat with each of the two side sections.

4 Cover the joined copper edges with flux, only doing a part at a time as it does evaporate. Solder along the seams using enough solder to form a bead as you draw the iron along each seam. Then tin (applying a flat surface of solder along the copper foil) all edges and the reverse side of the panel, too, remembering to flux it first.

5 Assemble the front and two sides, holding the lampshade together at the top and bottom with masking tape. Tack the pieces together with solder and leave to set solid. Finally, add the top in the same way.

6 Remove the masking tape and solder the seams. The easiest way to do this is to have the seam you are working on uppermost so that it is horizontal. This can be done by supporting the shade in a cardboard box. Apply enough solder to form a bead to fill in any cavities.

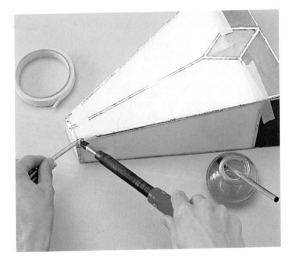

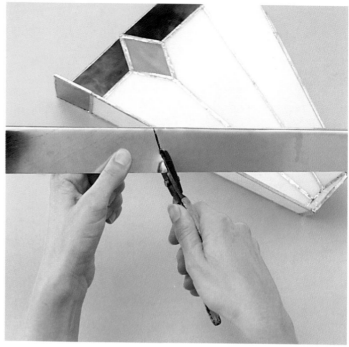

7 Tin solder the seams on the inside of the glass shade in the same way.

8 Place the tin plate bar across the back of the frame and mark where to cut it with a felt-tipped pen. Cut with tin snips and then flux and solder the piece of metal where it joins the glass at the edges for hanging. When the lampshade is finished, use warm soapy water to wash off any flux and oil residue from the glass. If you wish, the solder colour can now be changed to a copper colour with copper sulphate solution or to a lead colour with a black-it solution. Apply these patinas with a sponge, but always wear rubber gloves when doing this, and wash again with warm soapy water afterwards.

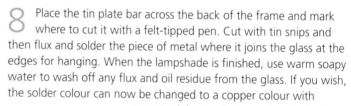

Outlines for the pieces of glass needed to make this lampshade. To make a shade the same size as the one featured here, enlarge these outlines on a photocopier by 400 per cent. You may have to make a copy at 200 per cent and then make a copy of the copy at 200 per cent as this is the enlargement limit on most machines.

Embellishments

There are many ways in which you can create your own lighting masterpieces from shop-bought lamps and shades. Most DIY places and department stores sell them at very reasonable prices — all you have to do is decorate them. You may choose to paint freehand, creating high art, or produce more humble effects with sponging, stippling, distressing, verdigris, lacquer or gold leaf. Or you may decoupage the shade or base, punch holes or cut shapes through a shade, embroider stitches or simply recover a shade to match existing decor. For those who like to be a little bit different, we have included in this section some wild ideas for decorating lamps using shells, glitter, driftwood, mock flowers or fruit, feathers and fringing.

opposite: There is a huge, almost unlimited choice of things to use for embellishing your lamps. From cords and tassels, to ribbons and lace, shells, sequins, buttons and bows, the list goes on and on.

Ribbons, buttons and bows

Accessories from your haberdashery drawer can come in useful if you want to create pretty and feminine shades for your home. Most sewing boxes are full of treasures, many of which may be used to decorate shades. These include buttons, ribbons, fringing, frogging, pompoms, sequins, piping, threads and fake flowers or fruit. You can blanket stitch, baste or hem around the edges of a shade using a brightly coloured string, wool or braid and change its appearance drastically. You may embroider or fake it with sewn badges which appear to have been embroidered, or you may appliqué or go for the no-sew approach with fabric and glue.

below: Plain lampshades have been punched at regular intervals along the upper and lower edges with a hole punch and then threaded with ribbons. *(Labeena Ishaque)*

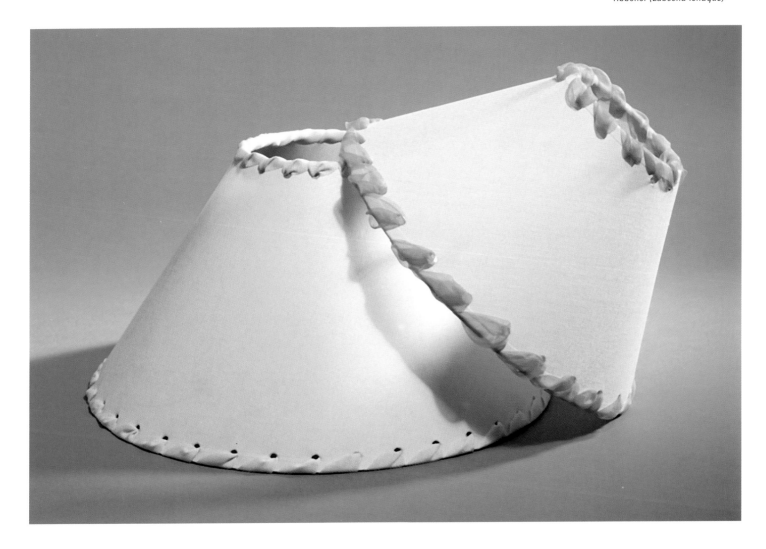

above: This shade already had green piping running along the edges so the colour was continued with the stencilling. Tartan bows were added at the bottom of each stencilled wreath. *(Charlotte Smith)*

above: The red piping on this shade was highlighted by attaching red and white gingham bows in a band around the centre. The bows have golden charms tied onto them with red cord. *(Charlotte Smith)*

left: A selection of embellished lampshades include ribbons, tassels, fake flowers and medallions attached regularly around previously plain shades. *(Charlotte Smith)*

Mixed media

The ordinary to the downright unusual items can be used for the purpose of decorating. The point is to decorate to your own tastes, whether they are conservative or innovative.

When decorating your lamps you can be as simple or as wild as your tastes dictate, look in shops and magazines for inspiration. See what you like and copy, adding your own personal details. Paint flames up the sides of the shade and base, cover it in padded hearts, attach key rings along the lower edge. It's your lamp and you can make of it what you will.

above: Fake flowers have been attached onto a stencilled pattern of flower pots on a shade. The stencilled leaves in the background have been cut-worked and pushed out, so the light will shine through clearly. *(Charlotte Smith)*

left: A shade and base have been treated with a trail of glue in swirly patterns and thick cotton cord stuck on. This idea can be used for any style or pattern. *(Jack Moxley)*

Using double-sided sticky tape, upholstery fringing was wound around the entire base and shade, to create a frothy and amusing look. Fabric glue would work equally well.
(Labeena Ishaque)

above: A white shade has been hemmed along the lower edge with a coarse linen thread, and small shells attached at every three or four stitches. The base was then painted with PVA to seal the wooden surface, layered with filler, and the driftwood and larger shells were stuck onto the tacky paste and allowed to dry.
(Labeena Ishaque)

far right: For this lampshade, scraps of scrim have been sewn together with a thick linen thread and frayed occasionally. Odd buttons and beads were sewn on in an irregular pattern.
(Juliet Bawden)

This esoteric lamp was created by wrapping a plain shade in fake grass and sewing on brightly coloured fake flowers. The base was painted to match and then wrapped in smaller fake flowers. *(Labeena Ishaque)*

above: A profusion of paper flowers in vivid coloured tissue papers have been glued onto a shade to give an Ascot hat of a lamp. *(Labeena Ishaque)*

above: A wicker lampshade was transformed with the use of a glue gun and a selection of delicious looking plastic fruits. The result was mouth-watering, with the plastic fruit glowing when the lamp is lit. *(Oliver Moxley)*

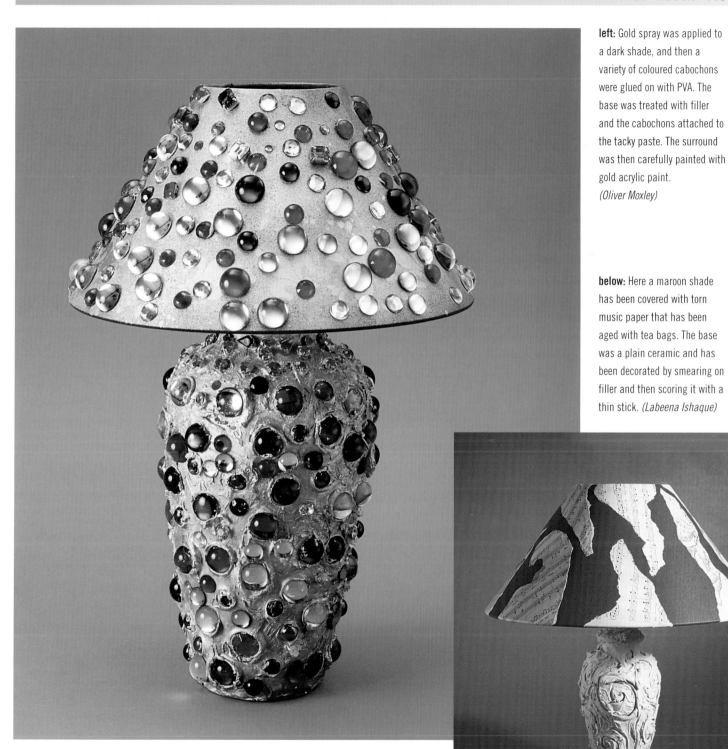

left: Gold spray was applied to a dark shade, and then a variety of coloured cabochons were glued on with PVA. The base was treated with filler and the cabochons attached to the tacky paste. The surround was then carefully painted with gold acrylic paint.
(Oliver Moxley)

below: Here a maroon shade has been covered with torn music paper that has been aged with tea bags. The base was a plain ceramic and has been decorated by smearing on filler and then scoring it with a thin stick. (Labeena Ishaque)

Papers and paints

Paper is something that absolutely everyone has in their homes and paint comes a close second. This means that using these things to embellish your lamps will be the most cost effective way to decorate them. Different ways of painting shades give very varied effects, especially when the lamp is lit. Stiff fabric or parchment shades are the usual kind found in department stores and the ideal paint to use on these is acrylic, because fabric and paper accept this paint easily and also because acrylics are available in a wide range of rich colours. Likewise, there are a great many different kinds of paper and there are so many ways to use them to decorate that it is impossible to list them all. But suffice to say that you will have things at home that you will be able to decorate your plain lampshades with.

above: A white pleated shade has been given stripes by painting every other pleat with black acrylic. The edges of the pleats were neatened by using a fine black felt-tipped pen. (Labeena Ishaque)

left: A stained old shade was disguised with lots of tea bag stains and gold acrylic paint applied in circular motions giving a golden and cloudy finish. Gold leaf was attached and then distressed with a fingernail. To finish it, stars cut from Japanese hand-made paper were stuck on. (Labeena Ishaque)

left: A cream lampshade has been stamped with potato prints in bright primary colours. The easiest shapes to cut are geometric ones like triangles, squares, circles and rectangles. The result is a simple and colourful child's lamp. *(Labeena Ishaque)*

right: Another stamped lamp is this one which has been stamped using a cork. The base was originally white but it has been painted red to contrast with the shade before stamping the motifs on top. *(Labeena Ishaque)*

opposite: A selection of paper candle shades. The one on the far left has been decoupaged with fake suede and stamped with gold fleur-de-lys. The other shades have been stencilled with vegetables and flowers. The two central candlesticks have been sponged to create a dappled effect. *(Charlotte Smith)*

left: This shade was painted royal blue and then made grand by gold paint sprayed through a doily to give a sharp and exotic finish.
(Labeena Ishaque)

above: Here a selection of flowers, leaves and vegetables, have been stencilled using plastic sheet stencils firmly attached to the shade to avoid slipping. The motifs have been painted with vibrantly coloured acrylic paints. *(Charlotte Smith)*

above: The decorations on this shade have been sponged through a stencil to give soft and patchy blue teapots. *(Charlotte Smith)*

Fabric

Remnants of fabric can be used to decorate shades to great effect. This is especially easy if the shade itself is fabric and sewing skills can be used to dress it up. Examples are given with these fabric shades by Heather Luke. Although made from the same pattern, the embellishments — embroidery, applique, silk flowers, braiding and ribbons — each achieve quite a different effect.

Silky fringing is added to a fine pleated lampshade to add detail to the lower edge.

Small lengths of chiffon have been rolled up and sewn together at one end to create roses. A succession of these has been placed along the top edge of the shade. *(Heather Luke)*

A strip of blue fabric with musical notes along the border has been folded in half lengthways and then sewn onto the top and lower edges of the shade to make a piping. The musical notes appear on the lower edge. *(Heather Luke)*

Add braiding that is either the same colour as the shade or one that enhances your decor.

Make a frill with a light fabric and sew it onto the brim, using a fine cord to disguise the stitches.

To add a variety of colours, attach some natural, thick fringing to the shade.

Sew on a longer fringe and cover the join with some narrow braid stitched over the top.

Gold, wired, iridescent ribbon is sewn onto the top and lower edges of the fabric shade. Note that because the ribbon is wired, it stiffens the gathers along the lower edge. *(Heather Luke)*

A plain cotton strip has been sewn along the lower edge of the shade and a matching thin ribbon tied into a bow at the top of the gathers. *(Heather Luke)*

Practicalities

Design considerations

There are basically three main areas of lighting to consider when planning a room. The first is a general, background light, then there is task lighting which allows for close work such as reading and writing and finally, there is accent or display lighting — most interiors will need a combination of all three. Lamps are a versatile, additional form of lighting, but it must be remembered that they are only a supplement to fixed lighting.

Overhead lighting creates a good general light and is more flexible if connected to a dimmer switch. This enables glare to be reduced and a soft and gentle atmosphere to be created; alternatively, if the switch is turned to almost maximum, a cool bright light results. Pendant lights hang down from the ceiling and the use of shades and bulbs can vary the quality of this light enormously. Uplighters provide a general background light and can be placed on the floor or wall. The light bounces off the ceiling spreading the light and reducing glare. When used low down, uplighters cast shadows and create dramatic lighting effects, especially if hidden behind objects or plants. Conversely, if placed higher, there is a greater intensity of light. Downlighters are more versatile, creating a variety of effects from a general light to task lighting. Today, recessed lights are commonly installed in interiors providing a good, unobtrusive light. Track lighting is equally popular and this allows more versatility than recessed downlighting although the designs available are rather unsubtle. However, the positioning of spotlights and the fact that it is easy to alter positions makes this an attractive choice whether used for specific tasks, such as lighting a painting or a piece of sculpture, or generally. Finally, there is the use of table lamps, wall sconces and even candles, all of which create a warmth or mood or can be used as task lighting as well as having the advantage of being easily moved or positioned.

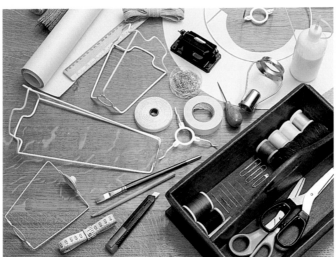

above: Some of the materials used in lampshade making. These include wire frames for the fittings, gimbals, tape, fabric measuring tools, scissors, craft knife and parchment.

Lighting for different rooms

The purpose and function of your room will normally dictate the kind of lighting you use. For example, an entrance and hallway, and particularly a flight of stairs, should be well lit to provide a welcoming glow and to prevent accidents. If your hallway is grand, it may benefit from a large central chandelier; if it is narrow, wall lights can make it appear wider. For a long, thin hallway, multiple light fittings and some points of interest such as paintings or posters which can be lit dramatically will help disguise its tunnel-like appearance.

The kitchen is often the hub of family life where everything takes place from food preparation to cooking, and homework or family meals. Different tasks, and times of the day, need different kinds of lighting. For example, a sink may be under a window and lit by daylight, but at night it will need to be lit to prevent working in your own shadow. Some kitchens have glass-fronted units which may benefit from display lighting for a special collection of, for example, china, or perhaps a dresser may need lighting. Worksurfaces are often lit by under-cupboard tube lighting with a light diffuser which allows the work surface to be lit without dazzling the person doing the preparation. A good idea is to have a flexible pendant light above the centre of the dining table, preferably with a separate switch, so that the table may be lit independently from the rest of the kitchen.

Living rooms are where lamps and shades come into their own, especially as far as creating mood is concerned. The texture, colour and the material used for making the lampshade, its shape and size and the type of bulb used will all have an effect on the atmosphere created. A lamp needs to look good unlit as well as lit. The colour of the shade can contrast or tone with the rest of the decor. When designing a living room, the background lighting will normally be chosen first and then task lighting added, such as reading lamps by a sofa or a lamp on a desk. If you eat in the living room you may want a central light over the table. Display lighting is the next consideration for lighting flowers or a fireplace, or pictures or wall hangings.

Bedroom lighting should be functional. You need to see to dress or at a dressing table, and to read in bed without disturbing your partner. It is also as well to be able to switch on one light from the door as you enter the room. Children's bedrooms may need a soft nightlight, but remember when choosing lamps for children's rooms, that safety should be considered at all times. Make sure that plugs are shuttered and lamps should be placed where they cannot be pulled over and should not be made of breakable materials such as ceramic or glass.

Lampshades

Lampshade frames are available in a wide variety of shapes and sizes. Most of the frames are very similar and are variations of the traditional coolie-shaped shade. The Empire shade, while still being a circular shape, varies in that the top edge starts higher than a coolie's, and it is also much larger. Then there are the hexagonal shades and the florals, which are a curved version of the hexagonal shade.

Selecting an appropriate shade

Lampshades need to look good whether the lamps are on or off. They either diffuse light or are opaque with the light escaping through the top or in a pool underneath. On a tabletop lamp, the shade usually echoes the shape of the base on which it is fitted, so that a square or rectangular base should have a panelled shade, while a rounded one should have a round shade. Narrow, tall shades are best suited to candle-shaped bulbs.

A rough rule to follow when selecting the shade is that the diameter at the bottom should be equal to the height of the base. A shade should cover the bulb and electrical fitting when viewed at eye level and remember that a bulb needs at least 12 mm ($\frac{1}{2}$ in) of space around it and if a 100-watt bulb or more is used, then allow at least 75mm (3 in).

Fixtures and fittings

When choosing fixtures for your shades, always follow safety precautions. Be sure that the bulb isn't too close to the shade; the minimum recommended distance is 3 cm ($1\frac{1}{4}$ in) between a 40-watt bulb and a paper shade. Never exceed the maximum wattage stated on the fitting.

Pendant fitting

Shades which are designed to hang will require a pendant fitting. These fittings are used domestically for general overhead lighting and they can also be used in tall standard lamps. The pendant fitting is an electrical fitting and floor-standing standard lamps are usually fitted with a duplex ring on which the shade rests.

Gimbal fitting

Table lamps use a gimbal fitting, which allows movement of the shade and these are available in various heights, altering the distance between the lamp base and shade. The gimbal is screwed onto the base directly below the bulb fitting, and it protrudes above the bulb. The shade supporting struts then rest in the valleys at the top of the gimbal. There is also a gimbal fitting for pendant shades called a spider gimbal which is a circular attachment that fits between the bulb fitting and the switch. Three arms are set equidistantly around the edges of the circular fitting and it is these arms that hold the pendant shade. A spider gimbal is usually used for tubular-shaped shades.

Bulb clip

Many table lamps and chandelier frames use a bulb clip which is a small, very adaptable metal attachment. It fits over wide and narrow bulbs and is especially ideal for using under small, lightweight shades.

Candle followers

These are shade holders for candles. They slot onto a straight-sided candle and support lightweight candle shades. They must never be left unsupervised because of risk of fire.

Choosing bulbs

Apart from the brightness or wattage, it may appear that all light bulbs are the same, but this is far from the truth. There are many different bulbs which produce numerous lighting effects. Bulbs are described in the following terms: lumens, watts, lumens per watt, life and colour.

Lumens is the unit that tells how much light a lamp will provide.

Watts is the rate at which the lamp will consume electricity.

Lumens per watt is a way of describing the efficiency of different lamps, in the same way as km (miles) per litre (gallon) is the way in which we describe a car's fuel consumption.

Life quoted for light bulbs is the average for that type. Although manufactured working to very close tolerances, those of the same type will not last exactly the same time.

Environmental factors such as supply of voltage, vibration and temperature will affect the life of a bulb.

Bulbs now come in a variety of colours, the most popular being white, and the requirement of white light varies depending on location. For example, a hotel will want a warm, welcoming white, whereas an art gallery will want a cool light to show off pictures accurately.

Light bulb availability
Normally, light bulbs come in either screw or bayonet fittings and are clear or pearl, but there are all manner of styles from which to choose.

Candle bulbs
Candle bulbs and small round bulbs are used for wall lights and multi-arm fittings, as well as in the classical chandelier.

Low-energy light bulbs
These are one of the most exciting and important innovations in light bulb design. They run a lot cooler than ordinary light bulbs and so are safer. Their life is also eight times longer than a normal light bulb and they use 75-80 percent less electricity. These bulbs are highly recommended for lamps. They should not, however, be used with dimmer switches or some timing devices.

Pygmy bulbs
This is the name given to low-wattage, very small bulbs used for hob lights, fridges or nightlights.

Softglow lights
These are pastel-coloured bulbs which come in a variety of colours and can be used to fit in with particular colour schemes.

Spotlights
Used around the home for directional lighting and for display, spotlights are ideal for downlights and work-lamps.

Materials for shades
There are so many materials to choose from for your lampshade that the list is endless. The only guideline is that the material must fulfil safety procedures in that the material should not be flammable. Paper and fabric should always be sprayed with flame retardant, which is readily available from theatrical suppliers.

When choosing material, hold it up to the light so that you can see whether it lets light through or not. Material which doesn't allow light through is fine, although material which does is probably a better choice as the light emitted will remain ambient rather than becoming a solid pool below the shade. Patterns, textures and colours all affect the kind of light the shade will give off.

If you are a beginner, paper and parchment are ideal as they are easier to handle than fabrics. The choice is huge, ranging from cartridge paper and hand-made tissue to old maps, wallpaper and gift-wrapping paper. Light, textured paper gives off a soft and interesting glow because the detailing on the paper is highlighted by the light passing through it. A darker and heavier paper will give a more subdued atmosphere. Plain papers can be detailed by scrunching up and flattening out again, pleating (see pages 44-7), layering, or cut-working using a craft knife (see pages 56-9).

Parchment and paper are also ideal for accepting paint so that you can stencil, stamp and sponge onto the shade. You can also decoupage onto them, apply transfers and even pierce the paper so that when the lamp is switched on the light shines through the holes giving an interesting effect (see pages 48-51).

With fabrics, again, the choice is massive. They are more difficult to work with than paper, however, as they don't hold their shape as well. As with paper, the kind of fabric you use will affect the kind of light given off. For example, a hessian or a fabric with a loose weave will give a dappled light as the light will show through certain sections and not others. Very light fabrics, like organza and chiffon, can be gathered (see pages 90-3) or pleated to create a very soft effect.

Trimmings can transform the plainest paper and fabric into fascinating and interesting shades. You do not have to decide immediately if you want to add any trimmings; it is probably easier to add them once the shade is complete. There are many trimmings to choose from including braids, fringes, tassels and piping. Raffia and strong threads and yarns are good because you can use them for decorating a shade as well as making a shade by winding the yarns all the way around the frame until it is completely covered.

Preparing a frame
Before making a lampshade, the frame needs to be painted to ensure that if rust occurs it won't stain the covering material. Paint also prevents the binding tape from slipping when the rings and uprights are bound. Binding is necessary so that there is a surface to which you can sew a fabric shade or glue a paper shade. Do not bind the wires that will eventually hold the shade to the light fitting. To estimate the amount of binding tape that is required, measure the length of all the wires, then allow 1½ to 2 times this amount of binding tape.

MATERIALS & EQUIPMENT

lampshade frame

sandpaper (fine grade)

damp cloth

enamel paint

paintbrush

lampshade binding tape

scissors

1 Sand every part of the metal frame with the sandpaper and wipe over it with a damp cloth to remove any dust. Then paint the frame with the enamel paint omitting those areas which will be in direct contact with the light bulb. Allow this to dry.

2 To bind the frame, cover both the top and bottom rings and each of the supporting struts with the binding tape. Bind the side wires first, leaving one unbound and then bind around the top ring, down the unbound wire and then around the bottom ring. To attach each length of binding, cut off a length of tape 1½ times the length of a strut, turn 2.5 cm (1 in) of tape over the top ring and down the strut. Then wind the binding diagonally over the overlap and down the strut to the bottom. Finish with a knot and trim off excess tape. Repeat for each part of the frame. When binding the top and bottom rings, make a figure of eight with the tape each time you come to a vertical strut.

Making a paper pattern

The first step in creating a lampshade is to make a basic paper pattern, which you can then use as a template for the material that you wish to use as a shade. A paper pattern can be used as a guide to mark and cut out the material, giving exact measurements and ensuring a good fit on the frame.

Although there is a wide range of lamp frames to choose from, the same basic method can be used to make a lampshade, whatever its shape.

MATERIALS & EQUIPMENT

lampshade frame

roll of lining paper or
a large sheet of paper

pencil · ruler

scissors · paper clips

PVA glue

1 Place your selected lampshade frame on its side at one end of the paper. Then roll the frame across the paper to ensure that there is sufficient paper. Once you have tested the size of the paper and you are sure it is large enough, place the frame back to the beginning.

2 Now roll the frame across the paper again. This time trace along the top and lower edges of the frame with the pencil, ensuring that you mark off the point of the frame where you started so that you will know when you have traced around the whole circumference.

3 After marking the top and lower edges onto the paper continue for another 1 cm (3/8 in) to allow for the overlap in the final construction of the shade.

4 Remove the shade from the paper and join the top and lower edges of the shade with a straight line. Cut along the pencil lines with the scissors.

5 Check that the pattern fits the shade by joining the ends with paper clips and then placing it over the frame. You are now ready to use the pattern on your chosen lampshade material.

Making a paper lampshade

Make a paper pattern and then follow steps 7 to the end of the Bonded coolie lampshade described overleaf.

Lining a paper lampshade

1 Using the paper pattern as a guide, cut the shade from your selected paper. Using a thicker paper as the lining, lay the lining on a flat surface.

2 Apply glue to the back of the shade and stick it down onto the lining paper, pressing down firmly to get rid of any lingering air bubbles.

3 Once you have done this, carefully cut around the shade and fasten in place as described from step 7 on in the Bonded coolie lampshade below.

Bonded coolie lampshade

A coolie lampshade is the most popular of shapes and is very straightforward to make. For the neatest finish, ensure you measure the frame most meticulously.

MATERIALS & EQUIPMENT

round lampshade frame

tape measure · rough paper · pencil

sheet card or stiffened paper

masking tape · compass · ruler

scissors · craft knife

clothes pegs · PVA glue

1 Measure the height (F to G on the diagram overleaf) and diameters (D to E and B to C) of each ring of the lampshade frame. On the piece of rough paper, draw a diagram as shown overleaf.

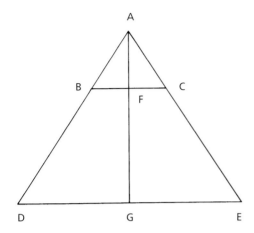

2 Lay the card or stiffened paper face down on a board and secure in place with pieces of masking tape. Measure the length of A to B on your diagram and set your compass to this length. (You may need to improvise and use a piece of string and a drawing pin to accommodate the length needed for drawing an arc.) Place the point of your compass at A and draw an arc on the card from point B to point C.

3 Repeat step 2 measuring the length from A to D. Then carefully draw another arc from D to E.

4 Measure the circumference of the lower ring of the lampshade frame adding 5 cm (2 in) where the seam will overlap. Use the tape measure to mark this dimension on the larger arc.

5 Use the ruler to draw two lines from A to D and A to E.

6 Cut out the card along the two arcs. Then, using the sharp craft knife and ruler, cut along the straight lines.

7 Using the clothes pegs to keep the card in place, fold the cut out card around the top of the lampshade frame. Use more pegs to keep the card in place around the lower ring. It will take time to achieve a

smooth, taut fit requiring you to remove the pegs and replace them several times until you are satisfied.

8 Draw a line down the edge of the inside of the card where it overlaps and remove the card. To neaten the overlap, draw a parallel line 1.5 cm (⅝ in) nearer the outside edge and cut along it.

9 Glue along the overlap and join the edges of the shade. Hold the overlap in place with clothes pegs and leave for an hour or more to ensure the glue has set.

10 Glue along the top edge of card and place it onto the frame using the pegs to ease it into position. Repeat this with the lower ring and keep the pegs in place until the glue has firmly set. Ensure the support wire of the gimbal is perpendicular to the seam of the shade.

11 Stick braid around the top and bottom edges of the shade to hide the raw edges.

Bonded drum lampshade
To make a drum-shaped lampshade, follow the instructions for the bonded coolie lampshade, but use a frame which has two rings with the same diameter.

Bonded fabric lampshade
Follow the instructions for the Bonded coolie lampshade, but before cutting out the card at step 6, stick fabric to the stiffened card, leave to dry completely and then cut out.

Sewn fabric lampshade
These instructions are for making a lampshade solely from fabric and require very simple sewing techniques. Bind the frame first as described on pages 122-3.

MATERIALS & EQUIPMENT

taped lampshade frame
tape measure
fabric · lining · scissors · needle
cotton · clear fabric glue
clothes pegs

1 Measure the circumference of the lower ring of the frame and the height of the frame. Double the circumference and add 5 cm (2 in) to all measurements for seams. Then cut the fabric and lining to these measurements.

2 For both the fabric and the lining, place right sides together and sew together the shorter edges 1.5 cm (⅝ in) in from the edge. Turn right sides out.

3 Along each long edge on both the fabric and the lining, sew a line of running stitches 1.5 cm (⅝ in) from the edge of the fabric and repeat with a parallel line 3 mm (⅛ in) nearer the edge. Secure one end of the cotton in each row and leave the other end free.

4 Place the material onto the frame and gently pull the threads so that the edge becomes the right size for the upper ring. Spread the fabric evenly around the ring so that the folds are the same size and equally spaced. Pin this onto the binding tape of the frame.

5 Repeat step 4 for the lower ring but remember that the gathers will not be so tight. Form the fabric into even folds by stretching it between the two rings, unpinning and pinning until you are satisfied with the appearance.

6 Trim excess fabric from both rings. Slipstitch the fabric to the taped rings.

7 Gather the lining in the same way as for the fabric and slipstitch it to the taped rings of the frame. When a strut is encountered, cut the lining material so that it fits around this part of the frame. Trim any excess lining as close as possible to the edge of the stitching.

8 To hide the raw edges of the fabric and lining materials, make a bias strip from the fabric. Cut a strip that is long enough to completely cover the circumference of each ring plus 2 cm (¾ in).

9 Press under 6 mm (¼ in) of the bias strip along the longer edge and attach this binding with the clear fabric glue. Use clothes pegs to keep the binding in place until the glue is set.

Tailored lampshade

For a neater finish make the lampshade cover and lining in two halves as described here. By stretching the fabric taught and then cutting it out you will end up with a beautifully tailored look.

MATERIALS & EQUIPMENT

taped lampshade frame

tape measure · fabric · scissors

dressmaker's pins · tailor's chalk

lining · needle · cotton

clear fabric glue

1 Measure the height of the lampshade frame and add 5 cm (2 in). Measure the circumference of the frame at its widest point and add 15 cm (6 in). Cut out the fabric using these dimensions and cut this rectangle in half across its length.

2 Pin one piece of the fabric to the taped frame starting with one upright and working half way around the frame. Stretch

the material between the uprights ensuring the fabric is taut. Then pin the material to the upper and lower rings, once again checking thoroughly for creasing.

3 With the tailor's chalk, mark the outline of the frame and carefully unpin the fabric.

4 Cut out the material along the drawn line adding 2 cm (¾ in) all around. Using this first panel as a pattern, cut out the other piece of outer fabric and then cut two panels of lining.

5 With right sides facing, pin, baste and sew together the outer pieces of fabric along the shorter edges. Press the seams and turn this tube of material right sides out. Repeat this with the lining material but remember to leave the seams on the outside.

6 Place the tube of fabric over the frame ensuring the seams are sited over two opposing struts. Pin this to the upper and lower rings making sure the material is taut.

7 Sew the fabric to the taped rings using doubled cotton and oversewing with small stitches. Trim excess fabric, cutting as close as possible to the frame.

8 Position the lining fabric with the right side facing inwards and ensuring the seams are again placed on the same upright struts as those of the outer fabric.

9 Pin the lining to the upper and lower rings, carefully snipping the material where it meets the gimbals. Ensure the lining is taut and oversew this to the outer fabric with the stitching on the outer edge of the shade. Trim excess material.

10 Cut out strips of lining material to 5 x 3 cm (3 x 1¼ in) and use these to neaten the points wherever the gimbals

meet the upper ring. Press under 6 mm (¼ in) of lining along the longer edge of each strip. Wrap these around and over the top of each gimbal and stick down well into place. Trim when dry.

11 To complete the lampshade, make a trim to neaten the top and bottom edges. Cut two strips of the outer fabric, one measuring the circumference of the upper ring and one measuring the circumference of the lower ring, adding 12 mm (½ in) to each. Both should have a width of 4 cm (1⅝ in). Press under 6 mm (¼ in) along the longer edges.

12 Stick the trim in place at the top and bottom of the shade. To neaten the join once you have worked around the edge of the shade, fold one end of the trim under by 6 mm (¼ in) and stick this on top of the end you started with.

Lining a fabric lampshade

If the material you decide to use is quite thin and flimsy and you don't want to make a fabric lining as described above, finish the shade professionally and simply by lining the fabric with an adhesive-backed plastic sheeting.

Take the cut fabric, turn in the edges and baste in place. Peel the backing off the plastic sheeting and smooth the fabric, wrong side down, onto it. Then cut around the shade outline and remove the basting stitches. Alternatively, use a piece of heavy card and then line the fabric in the same way as for a paper shade (see 123).

To attach a lined shade to the frame, first stick together the short edges of the shade and keep them firmly attached with paper clips. Then apply glue to the frame struts and slot the shade over the frame and press carefully but firmly into position.

Bibliography

Kevin McCloud's Lighting Book
(Ebury Press, 1994)

The Lampshade Kit
by Amelia St George
(Ebury Press, 1994)

The Lighting Book
by Deyan Sudjic
(Mitchell Beazley, 1985)

An Illustrated History of Interior Decoration
by Mario Praz
(Thames and Hudson, 1964)

Seventeenth Century Interior Decoration in England, France and Holland
by Peter Thornton
(Yale University Press, 1987)

Victorian and Edwardian Furniture and Interiors
by Jeremy Cooper
(Thames and Hudson, 1987)

Contributors and stockists

CONTRIBUTORS

Helen Baird
63 Laird House
Redcar Street
London SE5 0LT
Tel: 0171 252 5948

Michael Ball
Glyndale
St Mary's Lane
Ticehurst
East Sussex TN5 7AX
Tel: 01580 201015

Gore Booker
131 Kings Road
London SW3
Tel: 0171 376 7761

Caroline Bromilow
60 St Andrews Rd
Henley upon Thames
Oxon RG9 1JD
Tel: 01491 576605

Ben Comley
Unit 1
Cockpit Yard
Off Northington Street
London WC1 2NP
Tel: 0171 831 6212

Lilli Curtiss
401.5 Workshops
401.5 Wandsworth Road
London SW8 2JP
Tel: 0171 498 7045

Sarah Feather Design
Redwalls
Burley Woodhead
Ilkley
West Yorkshire LS29 7AS
Tel/fax: 01943 864500

Ann Frith
5 Chesham Street
Brighton
East Sussex BN2 1NA
Tel: 01273 625365

Clare Goddard
Studio 17
Cornwall House
21 Clerkenwell Green
London EC1R 0DP
Tel: 0171 251 3886
Fax: 0171 250 0297

Michael Hartley
71 Berry Street
Burnley
Lancs BB11 2LF
Tel: 01282 416461

Zoe Hope
Unit 5
Cockpit Yard
Off Northington Street
London WC1 2NP
Tel: 0171 831 6212

Rachel Howard Marshall
111 Dunstans Road
London SE22 0HD
Tel: 0181 693 0775

Eryka Isaak
12 Lickey Coppice
Cofton Hackett,
Birmingham B45 8PG
Tel: 0121 445 4559

Eva Bakkeslett
c/o Kroll Design
146 Columbia Road
Shoreditch
London E2 7RG
Tel/fax: 0171 739 9008

Andrea Maflin
50 Croftdown Road
London NW5 1EN
Tel: 0171 284 1224

Karen McBain
18 Widgeons
Alton
Hampshire
GU34 2JY
Tel: 01420 88377

Fiona McKeith
170 Brick Lane
London E1 6RU
Tel: 0171 377 0261

Jane Morrell
37 Groveburn Avenue
Giffnock
Glasgow
Scotland G46 7DA
Tel: 0141 638 7102

Helen Musselwhite
Unit 9
Goosey Wick Farm
Charney Basset
Wantage
Oxon
OX12 0EY
Tel: 01367 718778

Cheryl Owen
8 Makepeace Mansions
London N6 6HD
Tel: 0181 341 5644

David Page
c/o Rebecca Hossack Gallery
35 Windmill Street
London W1
Tel: 0171 436 4899

Jnr Phipps
158 Nimrod Rd
Streatham
London SW16 6TL
Tel: 0181 677 5928

Philippa M Rampling
284 RCR International Ltd
Pilot House
Kirby-le-Soken
Essex
CO13 0DS
Tel: 01255 677883
Fax: 01255 677998

Deborah Schneebeli-Morrell
10 York Rise
London NW5 1SS
Tel: 0171 485 4261

Debbie Siniska
Glyndale
St Mary's Lane
Ticehurst
East Sussex
TN5 7AX
Tel: 01580 201015

Charlotte Smith
55 The Rank
Maiden Bradley
Warminster
Wiltshire BA12 7JF
Tel: 01985 844561

Yuko Suzuki
7 Vaughan Rd
London
SE5 9NZ
Tel: 0171 733 3642

Karen Triffitt
Flat 2
237 South Lambeth Road
London SW8 1XR
Tel: 0171 735 0883

Unit Nine
Shed Eleven Studios
12 Plumptre Street
The Lace Market
Nottingham NG1 1JL
Tel: 0115 958 9136
Fax: 0115 978 5026

Melanie Williams
45B Lansdowne Drive
London E8 3EP
Tel: 0171 254 0012

Cate Withacy
Unit 2
Cockpit Yard
Off Northington Street
London WC1 2NP
Tel: 0171 831 6212

Lynette Wrigley
197 Hammersmith Grove
London W6 0NP
Tel: 0181 743 5700

Robert Wyatt
13 The Shrubbery
Grosvenor Road
Wanstead
London E11 2EL
Tel: 0181 530 6891

STOCKISTS

Dartington Pottery
Shinners Bridge
Dartington
Devon TQ9 6JE
Tel: 01803 864641
Fax: 01803 864163

Furniture Union
46 Beak Street
London W1
Tel: 0171 287 3424

Mr Light
279 Kings Road
London SW3 5EW
Tel: 0171 352 8398/7207

Papier Marché
8 Gabriels Wharf
56 Upper Ground
London SE1 9PP
Tel: 0171 401 2310

Shui Kay Kan
34 Lexington Street
London W1
Tel: 0171 434 4095

Chapeau Claudette Outlant
23 Alden Road
London SW17 OJT
Tel/fax: 0181 947 5521

Trait d'Union Lighting
16 Palmerston Road
London SW14 7PZ
Tel/fax: 0181 876 3778

Christopher Wray Lighting
Emporium
600 Kings Road
London SW6 2DX
Tel: 0171 736 8434

USEFUL ADDRESSES

With especial thanks to Fred
Aldous Ltd, British Home
Stores, Creative Beadcraft,
Homestyle Stores, Mazda
Lighting, Offray Ribbons,
Jacobs, Young and Westbury
Ltd and Liquitex who supplied
materials for this book.

A & J Lampshade Frames
42 Church Road
Mitcham
Surrey
Tel: 0181 848 6776

Fred Aldous Ltd
PO Box 135
37 Lever Street
Manchester 1 M60 1UX
Tel: 0161 236 2477
Fax: 0161 236 6075
*(Mail order. Craft materials inc.
lamp frames and decoupage)*

British Home Stores
Marylebone House
129-137 Marylebone Road
London NW1 5QD
Tel: 0171 262 3288
(Lamps and shades)

Creative Beadcraft
Denmark Works
Sheepcote Dell Road
Beaumond End
Nr Amersham
Bucks HP7 0RX
Tel: 01494 71560
(Carbouchons and beads)

Homestyle Stores
AG Stanley
Victoria Mills
Macclesfield Road
Holmes Chapel
Cheshire
Tel: 01477 544544

Jacobs, Young and
Westbury Ltd
Bridge Road
Haywards Heath
West Sussex RH16 1TZ
Tel: 01444 41241
(Raffia and lampshade kits)

Kansa Craft
The Old Flour Mill
Wath Road
Elsecar
Barnsley
S Yorks S74 8HW
Tel: 01226 747424
*(Stained glass suppliers;
mail order)*

Lampkits
16 Cliveden Road
Wimbledon
London SW19 3RB
*(Mail order. Send SAE for
details)*

Lead and Light
35A Hartland Road
London NW1 4DB
Tel: 0171 485 0997
*(Stained glass suppliers;
catalogue available;
mail order)*

John Lewis
Oxford Street
London W1
Tel: 0171 629 7711
(Suppliers of lampkits)

Lion, Witch and Lampshade
89 Ebury Street
London SW1W 9QU
Tel: 0171 730 1774
*(Lampshade re-covering
service)*

Liquitex
Binney and Smith (Europe) Ltd
Ampthill Road
Bedford MK42 9RS
Tel: 01234 3602201
Fax: 01234 342110
(Paints and brushes)

(Mazda), G E Lighting
Lincoln Road
Enfield, Middlesex EN1 1SB
Tel: 0181 366 1166

Offray Ribbons
Fir Tree Place
Church Road
Ashford
Middlesex TW13 2PH
Tel: 01784 248597

George Prior Ltd
49 Kingston Road
South Wimbledon
London SW19
Tel: 0181 540 6145
(Lampshade frames)

Panduro Hobby
Westway House
Transport Avenue
Brentford
Middlesex TW8 9HF
Tel: 0181 847 6161
(Extensive mail order catalogue)

Rougier & Plie
BP 492 - 91164
Longjumeau Cedex
France
(Shops/extensive mail order cat.)

South Africa
Art, Craft & Hobbies
72 Hibernia Street (opposite
Edgars)
PO Box 9635
George 6530
Tel: (0441) 74 1337
*(They offer a countrywide
mail-order service)*

Art, Leather and Handcraft
Specialists Shop
6 Musgrave Centre
124 Musgrave Road
Durban
Tel: (031) 21 9517

Craftsman
The Shop
10 Progress House
110 Bordeaux Drive
Randburg
Johannesburg
Tel: (011) 787 1846
Fax: (011) 886 0441

Crafty Suppliers
32 Main Road
Claremont
Cape Town
Tel: (021) 61 0286
Fax: (021) 61 0308

Mycrafts Shop (Pte)
Aliwal Street
Bloemfontein
Tel: (051) 48 4119

Southern Arts and Crafts
105 Main Street
Rosettenville
Johannesburg
Tel/fax: (011) 683 6566

PW Story (Pty) Ltd
18 Foundry Lane,
Durban
Tel: (031) 306 1224

Wardkiss Homecare
*(Branches throughout
Cape Town, Durban and
Westdene)*

Australia
Arts & Crafts Corner
34 Mint Street
East Victoria Park
Western Australia 6101
Tel: (09) 361 4567

BBC Hardware *Branches
throughout Australia, contact:*
Head Office Building A
Cnr Cambridge & Chester
Streets
Epping
NSW 2121
Tel: (02) 876 0888

Bunnings Building Supplies
(24 branches), contact:
152 Pilbara Street
Welshpool
Western Australia 6106
Tel: (09) 365 1555

Lincrafts Gallery
Imperial Arcade
Pitt Street
Sydney
NSW 2000
Tel: (02) 221 5111

Lincraft Head Office
For details of branches, contact:
103 Stanley Street
West Melbourne
Victoria 3003
Tel: (03) 9329 8555

Lincraft Shop
301, Pacific Fair
Broadbeach
Queensland 4218
Tel: (075) 723 800

Mitre 10 Head Office
For details of branches, contact:
1367 Main North Road
Para Hills West
South Australia
Tel: (08) 281 2244

New Zealand
City Lights Electrical
Queens Arcade
34 Queen Street
Auckland
Tel: (09) 366 6208

Coats Enzed Crafts
40 Sir William Ave
East Tamaki
Tel: (09) 274 0116

Dominion Paint Centre
227 Dominion Road
Mt Eden
Tel: (09) 376 6860

LA Irwin Ltd
Lamshade Frames
183 Captain Springs Road
Onehunga
Tel: (09) 636 8876

K Simpson Ltd
Powerhouse
48-50 Sale Street
Auckland
Tel: (09) 303 3136

Index